I0453956

Hypnotize Yourself

*For a Powerful Mindset
of Health, Happiness, and Success*

In 3 easy steps -

Learn to transform fears, anxiety, and bad habits into
confidence, courage & feeling great... and <u>much</u> more!

- What is your single greatest power? Page 8
- The 2 most important words you think or say? Page 17
- You will be hypnotized - Page 50
- Laugh your fears away! Page 77
- He overcame pandemic anxiety! Page 103
- She overcame claustrophobia! Page 106
- He improved his golf game! Page 108
- Public Speaking, Massive Confidence, Weight Control,
Socialize With Ease, Better Sleep, Stop Smoking and
Be Funnier! PLUS - 4 Self-hypnosis Scripts!

by 'The Happy Hypnotist' ™ Dr. Scarpati

Hypnotize Yourself for a Powerful Mindset of Health, Happiness, and Success
Copyright © 2024 by Dr. Scarpati

For more about this author please visit https://happyhypnotist.com/

This author is not engaged in rendering medical or psychological services, and this book is not intended as a guide to diagnose or treat medical or psychological problems. If you require medical, psychological, or other expert assistance, please seek the services of your own physician or mental health professional. Neither author or publisher are liable for any damages arising from or in connection with the use of any information within these pages.

All rights reserved. No part of this publication may be reproduced, distributed, or transmitted in any form or by any means, including photocopying, recording, or other electronic or mechanical methods, without the prior written permission of the author, except in the case of brief quotations embodied in critical reviews and certain other noncommercial uses permitted by copyright law. Please do not participate in or encourage piracy of copyrighted materials in violation of the author's rights.

No part of this book may be used for the training of artificial systems, including systems based on artificial intelligence (AI), without the copyright owner's prior permission. This prohibition shall be in force even on platforms and systems that claim to have such rights based on an implied contract for hosting the book.

I dedicate this book to you—*yes*, you, reading these words right now. You are someone who takes the initiative to journey within yourself to better understand how your mind works, becoming the best person you can be to naturally enjoy life and love every single day

Thank you!

I also dedicate this work to all of my clients from the past twenty-nine years who have had the courage to make a positive change for themselves and improve their lives.

TABLE OF CONTENTS

INTRODUCTION

*TO KNOW THYSELF
IS THE BEGINNING OF WISDOM.*
—SOCRATES

DO YOU SOMETIMES CONSIDER YOURSELF adventurous? Do you enjoy learning new ways to be successful? Of course! That is why *Hypnotize Yourself for a Powerful Mindset of Health, Happiness, and Success* is the perfect prescription for you. *Thank you* for choosing this book. I congratulate you on taking action by reading this hands-on approach to feeling great about controlling your mind, your habits, and your life.

Hi, I'm the Happy Hypnotist, Dr. Scarpati. For the past twenty-nine years, I've enjoyed helping people harness their infinite power to overcome fears, anxiety issues, negative emotions, defeatist thoughts, sad feelings, or bad experiences. They have learned how to move forward into greater fulfillment with healthy habits, happiness, confidence, and success. I *LOVE* my hypnotherapy and wellness/coaching work.

As you will learn in chapter five, millions of people have used hypnosis to improve their lives. Some notables you may be familiar with include Oprah, Ben Affleck, Tiger Woods, Drew Barrymore, Jessica Alba, Fergie, Lily Allen, Kevin Costner, Ashton Kutcher, Eva Mendes, Ellen DeGeneres, and Matt Damon to name a few!

You are going to learn self-hypnosis. What's self-hypnosis? It's a powerful tool for tapping into yourself by going inward to improve or update your personal program. And you might be happy to know that using self-hypnosis is going to be as easy as talking or walking.

Please understand this process is much more than just learning self-hypnosis. In three easy steps, I'll show you how to take total control of your mind and your life. First, you'll be educated on the basic truths of your mind. Second, you'll learn how to use proven mental success strategies. Third, you'll learn *self-hypnosis* (chapter five) by combining these elements. Blending these three steps is a powerful cocktail of guaranteed success and personal growth that will be positively life-changing.

Obviously, this book is for those who are ready to take control of their own minds and lives. We all know people who are not willing to take on this responsibility. You're going to learn some really cool stuff, because this book contains a treasure trove of knowledge and information that I use to help my clients become successful with their goals.

You'll have a front-row seat to see how professional hypno-therapists employ various techniques and tools to help people make positive changes. You'll see how my clients overcame public speaking fears, pandemic anxiety, claustrophobia, fears of driving a car, and they started feeling more confident in social situations. You'll learn techniques to say bye-bye to cigarettes, bad habits, and excessive eating. You'll discover how some childhood experiences may cause the adult mind to feel sad and insecure about anything—socializing, eating, even drinking water. It's OK if you're not initially familiar with some of the concepts. As you read, they'll become clear. You may notice a magnetic pull as to what rings true for you.

The chapters are presented sequentially to build upon each other. When you construct a house, the first step is always to complete the foundation. Therefore, each chapter will continue to expand your knowledge base. Be prepared for thought-provoking ques-tions and *valuable life lessons* on this trek that will draw you inward, resulting in knowledge, wisdom, and personal growth.

The early chapters reveal the laws of the mind or *the basic truths of the mind,* such as:

- What is your single greatest power?
- What are the two most important words you think or say?

This awareness will strengthen your mental building blocks for success and will assist you in a better understanding of your conscious and subconscious mind in relation to self-hypnosis.

As you read, look forward to these ten thought-provoking coming attractions:

1. Understanding your single greatest power
2. Discovering the number one trait of your mind
3. Learning the two most important words you think or say
4. Controlling and strengthening your internal dialogue (self-talk)
5. Understanding the difference between the subconscious and conscious and using proven methods to rewrite and reprogram the subconscious
6. Tapping into your personal power with self-hypnosis
7. Appreciating and accepting yourself and the people in your life
8. Guiding you to focus your mind on positive ways to achieve any goal, complete any task, let go of any negative habit, overcome any fear or anxiety, and feel calm and courageous in any situation
9. Feeling great about yourself, living a happy, productive, confident, and joyful life, and truly having the awareness that you have a *powerful mind*
10. Appreciating the value of laughter (especially in the bonus chapter) and having fun!

I will also share with you my life-altering epiphany, which was an instantaneous *aha* moment when I experienced a positive *life shift* that opened my eyes and my heart to a happier life. Other than that, it will just be an ordinary book. I was a former comedian, so don't be surprised if this journey is also fun. Yes, let's have some fun too!

A few things to keep in mind, please:

- You may notice that I'm intentionally repeating some concepts and ideas to maximize your comprehension. You may notice that I'm intentionally repeating some concepts and ideas to maximize your comprehension. (See what I mean?)

- It's OK if you don't find all the material to be a perfect fit. Simply gravitate toward what you like and what rings true for you.

As you read, ask yourself:

1. How can I use this information for my goals?
2. How can I benefit from this?
3. When can I start using these techniques and ideas?

This book will guide you through a three-step process of understanding the basic truths of your mind, using mental success strategies and combining these with *self-hypnosis*. You'll become your own hypnotherapist. I'm sharing decades of experience and knowledge to help you maximize your success and to live a happy and confident life, which you truly deserve.

In the pages ahead, you will cultivate new thoughts about yourself as you apply proven techniques for successful change. Whatever you would like to accomplish, using this life-changing information will assist in your success. If your goal is to feel great and smile more as you're working, playing, and socializing, then that will be your new reality. You'll hear your inner voice say, *Yes, I can do this.*

4

You'll also find a bonus chapter (addendum) in the back of the book. My life lessons, life challenges, and various employment experiences—some of which include working with several of the biggest names in the comedy business—are there for the taking. And there's the amazing story of how the universe guided me to become a hypnotherapist.

This is exciting! Let the knowledge flow as you see yourself grow, and let's begin.

Sincerely,

Dr. Scarpati
The Happy Hypnotist™

CHAPTER 1

WHAT IS YOUR GREATEST POWER?

CHANGE YOUR THOUGHTS,
CHANGE YOUR LIFE.
—LOUISE HAY

I love author Louise Hay's quote. She is one of my favorite writers—and it's true, as you'll soon discover.

Before we dive into hypnosis and self-hypnosis, the first two chapters will introduce you to step number one on this enlightening journey, which is understanding the basic truths of the mind. Basic truths could also be described as *laws of the mind.* This initial step will help you understand how your mind works. These truths are echoed by the world's top motivators like Tony Robbins, Zig Ziglar, Brian Tracy, Jim Rohn, and others. I teach my clients these basic truths because it helps them begin to see who's in control of their lives. It's also a perfect way to put your mind in gear for successful hypnosis.

Although our minds are powerful and complex, I believe the operation manual can be simplified. If you can easily operate a car, run a dishwasher, or color your hair, then you can just as easily direct your mind to feel happy, achieve your goals, and enjoy your life.

Stay with me on this. You know that to successfully drive your car—obviously, I'm *not* talking about electric cars—you need a certain type of gasoline, and, of course, you need oil for the engine. If your car requires regular gas, you're *not* going to put diesel fuel in it. True?

When you use your dishwasher, you need to add the proper cleaning agent before you turn it on. True?

You're *not* going to put gasoline in your dishwasher. True?

To color your hair, you would follow the instructions, mix the ingredients, set the timer, rinse, and you're done. You're not going to miss or forget a step. True?

I understand there may be some people who might not like this easy, direct approach of *Hypnotize Yourself for a Positive Mindset*, and that's OK. They can find another path forward. There are alternatives to just about everything in life. The tools and techniques I'm teaching have worked very well for myself and my clients.

For an optimal life, you need to understand the basics of how your mind functions. I've learned over the years that operating your mind can be as easy as driving a car, running a dishwasher, or coloring your hair. If you'd like to feel great and enjoy life, you just need to take control of the dial—or the control switch—of your mind. How you do this will soon become crystal clear as you discover your greatest power and the basic truths of your mind. You're going to love this book!

WHAT'S YOUR GREATEST POWER?

Don't tell me it's your ability to choose the fastest-moving checkout line at Walmart. (Although if this is your superpower, please share!) Typical responses have been honesty, sense of humor, faith, and so much more—all good qualities, but probably not *the* answer.

Here is your first basic truth, as illuminated in J. Martin Kohe's book *Your Greatest Power*, your single greatest power is your *power to choose your thoughts.* Yes, you have free will. You have the power to select any thought you want. We often forget this fact because our minds tend to respond and think in patterns that we've created. Thus, it may seem the power is *hidden* from us because we unconsciously follow the pattern.

Remember this—your greatest power to choose is always in the present moment.

Read that again. Really, read that again.

You're making choices all the time, consciously and subconsciously. There are more thoughts bouncing around between your ears than you can even imagine. Most thoughts you are not even consciously aware of. When you choose a thought, you're also choosing a feeling that will tag along with that thought. You may make bad choices, such as eating junk food, smoking, doing drugs, or not living up to your potential. Maybe you're choosing negative thoughts or emotions and not consciously aware of those either.

Try this, right now. Choose a thought of something you enjoy doing. Really, do this. What's an activity you enjoy? Whatever comes into your mind will work. You did it, right? Yes. More on this choosing power is coming up.

As you begin to acknowledge the fact that you have the power to select or choose your thoughts, you'll notice yourself being more consciously aware of your choices. Start paying attention to the type of thoughts you're having. This book will assist you in learning how to take control of your line of thinking. I love Eleanor Roosevelt's famous quote, "No one can make you feel bad about yourself unless you give them permission." She's reinforcing the fact that you have the power to make a choice.

Here's what you need to know: we think in patterns. According to *Discover Magazine* and TLEX Institute, you have about fifty thousand thoughts a day. About 95 percent of them are the *exact same thoughts* you had the day before. You read that right: 95 percent of your thoughts are the same as they were yesterday. You may have heard the expression, "We are creatures of habit." This explains it.

Although most of these thought patterns are out of your conscious awareness (hidden), they create the second basic truth of your mind. Are you ready for this second basic truth? *Your mind goes in the direction of its thoughts.* Another way of saying this is, "What you think about, you bring about." It's true. The target of your energy flow is the direction it will go.

Do you know what the placebo effect is? I am sure you have heard the term *placebo*. This is when someone receives a medical treatment that does not contain an active substance meant to affect health, but the person totally recovers and feels better. How does this happen? That is the power of the person's mind, also known as positive expectations. They expected to improve, and they did.

Motivational speakers, spiritual masters, hypnotherapists, and life coaches agree that what you hold in your mind tends to manifest. If you're constantly thinking negative thoughts, they become self-fulfilling prophecies. Obviously, it's important to hold positive, loving thoughts in your mind. Why? Your thoughts are creating your reality. Therefore, if you would like a positive reality, then choose your thoughts wisely. And, yes, this book is going to help you take control of this!

We're just getting started, and you've already learned two of the most important basic truths:

1. Your greatest power is choice.
2. Your mind goes in the direction of its thoughts.

Just being introduced to this knowledge will begin to help you become more aware of your hidden subconscious thoughts to develop a more conscious awareness. This will assist you in making good, positive choices.

Let's discuss the 95 percent habit pattern. Around 95 percent of our thoughts are the same ones we had yesterday. This configuration of your thoughts contains all your beliefs, your personality, and your self-image. Let's imagine it's a computer program.

How often do you update the software program on your computer? What happens when you don't update it? It runs slowly or might stop. Now consider your mind. If you continually set new goals and continue to learn and improve, you'll always be updating and enhancing your program. As adults, we tend to do things the same way we always have.

Has something like this next story ever happened to you? My lovely wife, Marilyn, and I were on vacation off the coast of Connecticut, at my brother-in-law Steve's house. It's a great place right on the water. I went to throw away some trash in his kitchen. I automatically opened the cabinet directly under the sink to discard it, because that's where the trash bin is in my own home. At Steve's house, the bin is in the cabinet *next to* the sink. While staying there, I made the same miscue a couple more times.

This simple example demonstrates how the mind works in repetitive patterns. It's as if the patterns are hidden because we're not consciously aware of them. It's OK that your mind works like this. Just make sure that your habits, your thoughts, and your programs are creating precisely what you want for yourself. My wife is happy that I'm programmed to take out the trash.

Perhaps now you understand why it's a challenge to make a change. Ninety-five percent of your thoughts are locked in a pattern. Some people have created negative thinking patterns, such as the following:

- I'm a loser.
- I'm unlucky.
- I don't deserve it.
- Nothing good happens to me.
- I feel trapped.
- I don't like myself.

11

You need to understand your thoughts just repeat themselves because our minds automatically run the programs we've created. The **GOOD NEWS** is that any configuration, any pattern, any program between your ears can be re-written and positively changed. The most important element is you; yes, YOU must want to make it happen. Understanding you have the power to choose by becoming aware of exactly what outcome you would like is your first step to success.

Now here is a good question for you: where do your mental habit patterns and beliefs come from? They're the result of how you perceived and internalized the various events and experiences that happened earlier in your life. This is obvious, right? Yes, how you personalized your experiences put into motion the creation of your behavior, your self-image, your personality, and your program.

Victor Frankl wrote *Man's Search for Meaning* in 1946. The book chronicles his experiences as a prisoner in a Nazi concentration camp during World War II, presenting incredible examples of using the power of choice under the direst of circumstances. Imagine death and destruction all around you. Frankl reported that conditions were so unimaginably horrible that he saw some of his fellow prisoners in this purgatory go into a corner of the room and curl up in a ball and just die. However, some in the same circumstances made a different choice. Some chose to have a reason to survive, a purpose. Whether it was a choice to see their loved ones in the future or to get revenge against their captors, they had a purpose.

How about that? Some *made a choice* to have a purpose while they were surrounded by torture, forced labor, unsanitary conditions, and almost no food and death. Frankl chose to make it his mission to tell the world about the cruelty he and his fellow prisoners endured while living in hell on earth. *Man's Search for Meaning* is the result of his choice. You may want to choose to read it.

Please put your entire focus on this next sentence. If Frankl could exercise the power of choice to create a positive purpose under those conditions in a concentration camp, you—yes, *you*, reading these words right now—can surely do it under normal living conditions. Right? Yes, absolutely you can! You're now learning to be more aware of your thought choices.

When I was in acting school, we would be directed to express an emotion in an acting scene. At the time, it never occurred to me that I was using my greatest power to choose. Let me explain. I studied method acting at Lee Strasberg Theatre & Film Institute in New York City. The professors taught us to memorize lines without injecting emotion. You repeat the lines like a robot until they're locked in your mind. Then, right before your performance, you go off to the side for about fifteen minutes and recall a personal experience that will bring up an emotion related to the scene. If your lines require you to feel sad, you zero in on that sad feeling and let it wash over you. Then, when you start acting, the emotion blankets your words and makes your performance more realistic. The result is that you create an emotionally charged scene.

If you can *choose* to feel sad, angry, or any other emotion for the purpose of acting, then why can't you make a choice to feel calm, happy, or confident simply because you would like to? You can!

The choice is yours. Right now, make a conscious choice to think about something that makes you feel happy or loving. Let's do this again. Take a deep breath in through your nose, fill up your lungs, and exhale slowly through your nose. Let something come into your mind that makes you feel happy or loving. Maybe it's a happy memory from your younger days with a parent or grandparent. Maybe it's a Christmas memory. Maybe it's just the free feeling you have when you're riding your bike or on a beach looking out at the ocean. Maybe it is just being in nature that creates a happy feeling. Let some good-feeling thoughts flow into your mind, loving or happy. Do it now!

Please stay with that positive vibe.

Ahh, see how nice that is? These feelings you've just created are not only pleasant, but they're very good for your health and well-being. I may be dating myself with this next reference, but as the Beach Boys sang, "Gotta keep those lovin' good vibrations a-happenin'."

If I were to write the owner's manual of the mind, my very first instruction would be:

Your mind creates thousands of thoughts a day, and *you're responsible for your thought choices.* Forget about any past mistakes or past events. Today is a new day. For optimum use, select positive, happy, loving thoughts, and you'll have a happy, positive, loving life.

Warning! Warning! Choosing negative thoughts will lead to un-necessary, unhappy feelings.

I know this sounds simple (and there may be some people who reject the idea, and that's OK), but as you'll see, it's true. Once you train your brain to live in the moment and let go of past ex-periences that you categorized as negative, hurtful, or sad, you'll feel great and really enjoy your life every day.

We are human beings, so life is going to happen. I received a phone call in August of 2021 that my daughter, who was 4 months pregnant at the time, was in a horrific car accident. When I got the news, my body exploded with emotion and in a short while I started praying and taking some slow breaths to calm myself. Thankfully, everything turned out fine and our grandson is now three years old.

The message we are focusing on is our day-to-day attitude or mindset. When you wake up in the morning, what are your first thoughts? Are you reaching for your phone to get on social media or checking your email? Are you getting ready for the same bev-erage you always have in your favorite mug? Is your mindset, *This is going to be a good day*? Become aware of your routine thoughts and actions. Make sure they're truly serving you and your goals.

Three facts to review:

1. You have the power to choose your thoughts.
2. Your mind works in repetitive patterns.
3. The mind *goes in the direction of its thoughts*, and what you hold in your mind tends to manifest; therefore, keep it on the positive track.

Just being introduced to this information, you'll start to see yourself being more aware of your thought choices. You're going in the direction of your thoughts. Right now, you're going to read chapter two. What do you think are the two most important words you think or say?

Hint: they aren't *Häagen Dazs*.

CHAPTER 2

WHAT ARE THE TWO MOST IMPORTANT WORDS YOU THINK OR SAY?

WHETHER YOU THINK YOU CAN, OR YOU THINK YOU CAN'T, YOU'RE RIGHT.
—HENRY FORD

As you read this chapter, you may begin to notice your personal power improving. Before you learn the two most important words, I have some questions for you:

- Would you like to create some new healthy habits?

- Would you like to sleep better?

- Would you like to improve yourself in a sport or activity?

- Would you like to feel stress-free and more confident?

- Would you like to have the ability to transform how you feel about a negative experience?

- Would you like to see yourself feeling great every day and enjoying your life?

If you answered yes to any of these questions, and you have grasped the concept that your thoughts guide your life, then you're ready for chapter two. Remember: what you focus on is the direction in which you go. What you think about, you bring about.

Right now, your thoughts are focused on learning and understanding the information in this book. Very good. I like that. Now, what are the two most important words you think or say? Want to take a guess?

The two most important words are...

Wait for it...

I am.

Yes, *I am.*

Whatever follows "I am" is something *you* are going to live up to or down to.

"I am" has been around for so long that it can be found in biblical references. In the Gospels, *Ego eimi* translates as *I am.* We already know that you move in the direction of your thoughts, so stop saying anything negative after "I am," even in a joking manner. Never say, "I am a jerk" or "I am a stupid idiot." No, no, no! From this moment forward, say only positive things about yourself. If you make a mistake or offend somebody, it's OK. Just say, "I'm sorry," learn from it, and move on by following up with, "I'm going to do better."

Keep your "I am" statements positive. Here are ten good examples:

- I am a considerate person.
- I am a good friend who's interested and supportive of others.
- I am the type of person who sets good goals for myself.
- I am a good listener.
- I am a friendly person who's also helpful.
- I am intelligent.
- I am a hard worker.
- I am a good sister/brother.
- I am focused on healthy choices for myself.

- I am the type of person who can challenge myself.
- I am the type of person who does not have to be perfect *but strives for improvement.*

Do you get the idea? Always, *always* frame yourself in the positive. Make sure that what comes after "I am" is something you truly want.

You're now learning and using positive, powerful, life-changing laws of the mind. Isn't that wonderful? Yes, yes, and *yes*!

Just as vital, pay attention to what follows *I* in any statement you might make, and always keep a statement positive. Here are ten good "I statement" examples:

- I respect myself.
- I respect others.
- I have great goals for myself.
- I love myself.
- I love others.
- I love learning and improving.
- I enjoy being with other people.
- I accept myself.
- I can let go of the past.
- I accept others as they are.

This logic also applies when using the word *my*. Occasionally one of my clients will say, "Well, my addictive behavior will make it so hard for me to stop smoking (or doing drugs, having temper tantrums, eating junk food, practicing unhealthy sexual behavior, or binge-watching sitcoms)."

If you believe that you have an addictive personality, you can still move forward in a positive way. Here are some ways to phrase or frame positive intentions:

- My addictive behavior is now focused on eating healthier.
- My addictive behavior is now focused on being a considerate person.
- My addictive behavior is now focused on taking great care of myself.
- My addictive behavior is now focused on learning new information and improving.
- My addictive behavior is now focused on making new friends.
- I think you're getting the idea. Focus on framing *everything* in a positive way.

Another term used to describe the "I am" concept is *self-talk*, which is also known as your *internal dialogue*. This internal dialogue is made up of the thoughts that you have between your ears. Remember: humans have fifty-thousand thoughts running through our heads each day. Obviously, these thoughts create your self-talk, so why not keep them happy, positive, and loving?

Mastering these "I am" tactics will strengthen your focus and keep the negativity out. Your job, *your responsibility,* is to make sure that whatever follows *I am*, *I*, or *my* is something you truly want.

Life Lesson: Pay attention and take positive ownership of your "I am." Read that again, please.

Nice work! You've just completed step one of taking control of your mind and taking control of your life. Step two is straight ahead in chapters three and four. Be ready to experience a few important self-talk tips.

CHAPTER 3

STRATEGIES TO STRENGTHEN YOUR MIND

A VISION WITHOUT A STRATEGY REMAINS AN ILLUSION.
—LEE BOLMAN

THIS CHAPTER AND CHAPTER FOUR are step two in this learning process. Hypnosis will be coming up, but learning, understanding, and experiencing these initial chapters first is best, because they totally prepare us for step three. Be ready for many easy-to-use but powerful mental strategies that you can utilize right now. These mental exercises are not only fun and interesting, but they'll help you keep the spotlight on your thoughts, which will thus strengthen your internal dialogue to help you shift and maintain a positive path.

Your internal dialogue (self-talk), your narrative, is what you say to yourself every day. When I was younger, some of my narrative was more like, *I don't think I can do that. I'm not sure if I'm smart enough or good enough for that.*

Everything started to change once my self-talk switched to asking myself different questions such as, *how can I do that? What do I need to do to make that happen?*

I've heard someone refer to our self-talk as our inner world, vs the outer world. The reality is everything, yes everything is in our inner world! The techniques you will be learning shortly will strengthen your inner world.

Have you ever known someone who always plays the victim? Nothing ever goes right for them. They blame everyone else for their problems. No one has it as bad as them. This person has not realized yet that they simply need to change their story. If you're the person who always plays the victim—thinking nothing ever goes right for you—right now you may think *but you don't know what it's like to be me!*

Just keep reading.

You are about to acquire knowledge of seven proven techniques that are going to help you build a powerful and positive inner world, self-talk. You need to understand how vitally important it is to be in control of your personal narrative. *It's nonnegotiable. You must learn to harness your own personal power now, and you will.* These affirmation techniques will not only also assist in your self-hypnosis journey, they'll improve your self-talk, and the end result is a healthier and stronger and confident you. After reading each tip, please consider how you might use them. Then, *imagine* yourself using them.

SELF-TALK TIP 1: AFFIRMATIONS

I'm sure you've heard about affirmations. In self-help work, an affirmation is a positive statement you say or think about your goal. The purpose of using affirmations is to help keep you focused on your goal because what you hold in your mind tends to manifest. An example for someone who wants to be a nonsmoker might be, "I choose to be a happy nonsmoker."

Let's say your goal is to control your weight. One of your affirmations may be, "I now eat less, and I only eat healthy foods. I can do it."

Or if you're a sugar addict, the affirmation may be, "I say *no* to sugar poison. I only put healthy foods in my mouth. I can do it."

Come up with a couple of positive affirmations you can use for yourself. Write them down. It's OK to use any of the ones I listed.

Author Louise Hay, who I *love*, said, "Anything you say, or think is an affirmation for yourself." This is true, which is why you must keep your thoughts positive. So, it's suggested that you repeat your positive affirmation many times throughout the day. First thing in the morning and before bed are excellent times to work with your affirmations. Now imagine yourself using this technique. Yes, do this now, please. Visualize yourself getting ready for bed and repeating your positive affirmation.

SELF-TALK TIP 2: FIVE-MINUTE WRITING, PRINTING, AND SPEAKING

Pick up a journal or notebook to use for this exercise. I love this technique of writing your affirmation. It helps speed up success because the act of physically writing on paper develops a stronger, deeper conceptual understanding as opposed to just typing. Take five minutes each morning and put pen or pencil to paper and write out your affirmation. First, write your affirmation in cursive, and then say it out loud! Then, print your affirmation and say it out loud. Then, back to cursive and repeat! Do this for just five minutes every morning.

SELF-TALK TIP 3: "THAT'S LIKE ME."

In Denis Waitley's book, *The Psychology of Winning,* one of the main themes is that when you see someone demonstrating positive behavior that you would like to emulate, tell yourself, "That's like me."

Or if you want to feel more confident, think of who represents the style and type of confidence you would like. This can be a real person you know or even someone in the media. As you imagine this person, say the words, "That's like me."

I understand that it may seem strange at first, but you'll notice as you use the technique that it will yield results. When you notice *yourself* acting in a positive way, again say, "That's like me."

Continually aligning yourself with positive, admirable behaviors will keep you going in the right direction. Now take a moment to think about when you might use this technique. Please write it down.

Now imagine yourself using this technique.

SELF-TALK TIP 4: REMOVE WEEDS

I love this next metaphor because it's a helpful visual as well as a very good technique. Picture your mind as a beautiful garden. Imagine any weeds that appear are negative thoughts. You know what happens when a garden is overgrown with weeds? The weeds block the sun and suck up nutrients from the soil, which smother the energy required to grow beautiful plants and flowers. Negative thoughts are the killer weeds that can choke the energy and life force out of your brain. You need to weed your garden occasionally. Keep your life weed-free, clean, and positive. You can do it.

Thinking positive and loving thoughts fertilizes beautiful flowers and plants in the garden of your mind.

Please take a moment now and inhale a slow deep breath in through your nose. Then exhale the breath slowly. Take another slow deep breath, fill your lungs, and let it out slowly.

Notice what comes up when you ask yourself, "Do I have any negative thoughts about myself?" Whatever comes up, that's what you may choose to work on.

Pretend you're standing in a beautiful garden that represents your mind. Close your eyes and imagine you're in this lovely garden; you may even sense the fresh smell of the garden. Look around. Do you notice any negative weeds? Now imagine yourself reaching down and pulling the weeds out. As you do this, allow yourself to feel positive about taking control and removing these pessimistic or negative thoughts. It's a good vibe to yank out the negativity.

Take a minute and do this now. Imagine you're weeding your garden to make it look positively beautiful.

SELF-TALK TIP 5: "I CANCEL THAT."

Here's another way to help realign your thought process and keep negativity out. Anytime you catch yourself or notice a negative thought, say, "I cancel that." Then, instantly replace the negative thought with a positive or happy thought.

Another way of doing this is to imagine that you're observing yourself from above, watching how you think. Your thoughts are inside a speech balloon. When you see a negative thought, you say, "I cancel that," pop the balloon, and change it to a positive thought—any positive thought.

For example, let's say you have a speech to give tomorrow, and the thought appears, "I'm so nervous to give my speech tomorrow." Immediately say, "I cancel that and pop that negative balloon," and replace it with the statement, "I have put in the work, and I feel confident to present my ideas tomorrow, and I'm looking forward to it." Or replace it with *any* happy or positive thought.

Again, when you notice a negative thought, just say, "*I cancel that*," and replace the thought with anything that is positive. As you continue to do this, you'll notice that the negative fades away because you've trained your brain to be powerfully positive.

SELF-TALK TIP 6: ADVERTISE TO YOURSELF

I love this one! Advertising companies know that one of the keys to success is having their message in front of you. The more times you see a commercial, the more the advertisement increases the likelihood of using the product or service. You can advertise to yourself by placing messages about your goal statement in front of you.

Create an ad campaign to yourself. I have seen this technique successfully used for healthy eating, feeling calm, being a non-smoker, and so on. Post-it notes work perfectly. Write your goal statement or one of your "I am" affirmations on a note and place it on your bathroom mirror, nightstand, car dashboard, refrigerator, computer screen, the back of your phone, or inside your wallet—any place where you'll see it. Every time you see the advertising to yourself, it'll be positive and helpful. This works!

You want to stop smoking? Write on Post-it notes "I'm a happy nonsmoker!" and put them in all the obvious places. This will initially help remind you and make it easier for you to say no to cancer sticks. This technique has helped so many of my clients over the years.

You want to cut out sugar? Write on Post-it notes "Sugar is poison. I say NO to poison." If you would like to feel more confident, write on Post-it notes "I accept life's challenges. My confidence is growing stronger every day."

Anthony, thirty-seven, used the "advertise to yourself" technique when he ended a bad relationship. Although not typical, I thought his approach was unique and creative, so I'll share it. He was engaged to be married, but the relationship had a pattern of running hot and cold. It would be hot and heavy for a while, and then they would get into a fight, make up, and run the same negative pattern over and over. He realized this was not what he wanted, and after repeated attempts to escape this pattern, he realized he had to end the relationship. It was very emotional, but he knew this action was the best decision.

Once he chose to end the relationship, he wrote an affirmation—"the best decision of my life"—to help remind him that this was a good choice of action. He posted the message in all the obvious places. He also stuffed them in places that he would come across much later, such as the inside of his dresser drawers, the glove compartment of his car, the freezer, desk drawers, filing cabinets, and inside some books on his shelf. Two years later—yes, two years later—he found one of the notes in his garage, where he had left it on the corner of the shelf. He laughed out loud when he found it and said, "Yes, that was a great decision!"

He ended up meeting the woman of his dreams. Ten years later, he's happily married to the love of his life, and they have two beautiful children.

SELF-TALK TIP 7: SEMINAR LEADER TECHNIQUE

As a former schoolteacher, I know this really works! It has been scientifically proven that when you teach something, the information, the concepts, and the nitty gritty become more personal and more embedded into your mind. Obviously, you learn the topic and comprehend it at a deeper level. This powerful seminar leader technique has you imagine yourself teaching a class on the *laws of the mind.* You imagine yourself standing in front of a class, describing your single greatest power—the number one truth of the mind—and the two most important words you think or say.

Use chapters one and two to help yourself create a lesson plan for this exercise. Then close your eyes and envision yourself confidently standing in front of a group of people discussing and teaching the basic truths of the mind. You may envision yourself writing the following questions on a whiteboard:

- What's the number one truth of your mind?
- What's your single greatest power?
- What are the most important two words you think or say?

Imagine the class is enthusiastically watching and listening as you enjoy teaching the lesson.

I also suggest you play with these seven self-talk tips. Try them all and gravitate toward what feels right for you in your current journey. These exercises will build positive internal dialogue and keep you focused on your goal. Imagine yourself applying these helpful approaches:

1. Use positive affirmations.
2. Practice five-minute writing, printing, and speaking.
3. When you see a positive action, say, "That's like me."
4. Remove negative weeds in the garden of your mind.
5. Negative thoughts say, "I cancel that." Replace negative thoughts with something positive.
6. Advertise to yourself.
7. Act as seminar leader.

Enjoy working with all of these techniques. I recommend incorporating them into your game plan for achievement. Feel free to experiment with them anyway you would like.

Life Lesson: Make sure all of your language is positive and reflects what you truly want for yourself. Take positive control of your self-talk!

Coming up next is the single strongest technique to de-stress. It's so powerful that it requires its own chapter.

CHAPTER 4

EASY INSTANT STRESSBUSTER

*THE GREATEST WEAPON AGAINST STRESS
IS OUR ABILITY TO CHOOSE
ONE THOUGHT OVER ANOTHER.*
—WILLIAM JAMES

THE STRESS-BUSTING TECHNIQUE YOU'RE ABOUT to learn is so powerfully important, it deserves its own chapter!

We all experience a little stress occasionally. This would be considered normal. In today's fast-paced world, though, a lot of people report they're *totally* stressed out. Some forty million American adults experience anxiety disorder. The amount of prescription medication that doctors hand out for stress-related issues rises each year. Now you can start reversing that trend by learning how to use this natural stressbuster, *and it may even save you a co-pay!*

Not all stress is bad for us. It is beneficial when we exercise and put some physical stress on ourselves. This chapter focuses on what I call *mental stress*, the feeling of being overwhelmed with something that leads to nervousness, anxiety, and fearful thoughts.

YOUR NERVOUS SYSTEM

First, let's briefly discuss your nervous system. It has two main parts: the sympathetic and parasympathetic nervous systems.

Both parts are important for modulating many vital functions, including respiration and cardiac contractility (your heartbeat). There is a natural, healthy balance that should be present. The *sympathetic system* initiates the fight-or-flight response, and the *parasympathetic system* initiates the rest-and-digest.

As you may know, if you're being chased by a tiger, your sympathetic nervous system is in full gear, accelerating the adrenal glands and giving your muscles the needed blood supply so you can escape without being lunch for the tiger. The parasympathetic system takes a bit of a back seat during such times.

But consider this: when was the last time you were being chased by a tiger? In today's world, at some level, it may seem like it wasn't very long ago. In fact, for many of us, our sympathetic nervous system is constantly engaged. Why? Many people report feeling stress from chasing deadlines, road rage, financial concerns, busy schedules, relationships, children's issues, or what someone said about them, and so on.

Many of us feel a sense of stress when something is not done yet, or unfinished, such as a decision that needs to be made or housework we need to do before company arrives. It could be an unresolved relationship issue, or maybe just responding to an email or phone call. These are examples of something unfinished. Some of us may experience a little churning in our gut, develop headaches, fatigue, muscle aches, and pains. This technique you're about to learn will definitely help you in these areas.

Multiple studies report that feeling chronic, sustained mental stress and anxiety day after day, week after week, is constantly activating your sympathetic nervous system, which is a sure recipe for disaster. Experiencing constant stress overworks your adrenal glands, thus causing a cortisol and hormonal imbalance. This imbalance brings on various health issues, including fatigue and an out-of-balance, weakened immune system that makes you more vulnerable to viruses and bacterial infections. Even if the COVID virus had never existed, we would still need healthy immune systems. It's important to note that you can keep your immune system healthy by practicing stress reduction techniques, eating a healthy diet, getting adequate sleep, fresh air, and sunshine. And above all, exercising can really help manage stress and anxiety.

If you ever watch the TV channels Animal Planet or Discovery, you might see an animal being chased by a predator. After the long pursuit, if the animal runs free and finally comes to a stop, you may notice that their body is visibly quivering. This physical reaction is a result of their nervous system rebalancing. The ability to reboot the nervous system is a natural response that some animals must use to relieve stress and trauma, which is good news! Humans can rebalance our nervous systems too, without taking drugs. I call it the *stressbuster!*

Just wait until you see how easy this is going to be. This simple technique has been around for a long, long time. To reset your nervous system, all you need to do is some slow, deep breathing through your nose. When you breathe in, ensure that your diaphragm fills with air, slowly expands, and then releases. Allow the abdomen to contract at the end of exhale, emptying the breath.

In contrast, have you ever noticed how you're breathing when you're stressed? The answer is that it's shallow chest breathing, and by countering that with slow, deep breaths, you'll automatically put your mind and body back on a healthy track.

Several studies have proven that taking the time to focus on controlling your breathing (meditation) has amazing benefits to your overall health, your immune system, and even your cognitive functions. What you eat also effects your nervous system. Consider this an important reminder that sugar and highly processed foods are very detrimental to the parasympathetic nervous system as well as your entire health. I'd like you realize that sugar and ultra-processed food are equally as bad for our health and well-being as negative thoughts.

THE STRESSBUSTER TECHNIQUE

Let me first tell you the breathing technique. Second, I'll go over each step. And third, you can do the technique.

If you're feeling stressed, you'll use this breathing technique. It will shift how you feel because this type of breathing restores calm and balance. This will guide you into the *parasympathetic system.*

Get into a comfortable position and become aware of the present moment, noticing how your body feels against the chair or sofa you're in. Imagine the muscles in your body are just letting go and softening. Take a deep breath in through your nose, using your diaphragm as you inhale, and fill your lungs as deeply as you can. Next, still holding that breath, take a second breath, inhale again, and grab a little more air to fill up your lungs completely. Hold the breath for a few seconds and let it out slowly through your nose. Now allow the breath to easily flow in and out of your nose. Your goal for now is to keep an even ratio as you inhale and exhale through your nose. To begin, inhale to the count of three or four, and exhale to the count of three or four. Do whatever feels most comfortable. Later, we can expand it to the count of five or more. Every study has affirmed that *nose breathing* is optimal for meditation. I'd like you to read the following steps first, and then we will do it.

1. Get comfortable, inhale as deeply as you can, and hold your breath for a second or so. Then, try to breath in again, taking in even a little bit more air, and hold for a few seconds. Then, exhale, pushing out all the air and emptying your lungs.

2. Continue taking breaths through your nose to the count of four on the inhale and the exhale. With each breath, use your diaphragm, feel your diaphragm expand, and let the air fall deep into the belly. As you begin to work with this, you may want to expand your count to five. For now, you just want to keep the inhale and exhale even.

3. Place all your attention on breathing in and out through your nose with an even count. Stay with whatever count— three, four, or five—feels more comfortable. If your mind wanders off for a second or so, that's ok, just refocus.

Performing an even count on the inhale and exhale signals your parasympathetic nervous system to initiate calming of the body and mind. As you continue with an even count, you'll soon notice that you start to calm down. Think of this breathing pattern as a dial that you can use to reset your body to the parasympathetic mode.

Some people feel comfortable with a five count in and out. As you practice and experiment, see what works best. Some prefer to count out loud and may even say the numbers, as in, "One thousand and one, one thousand and two, one thousand and three, one thousand and four," instead of just saying, "One, two, three, four." Using the thousand count may help some of us slow down. It's important and beneficial to *do the count at a slow, steady pace.*

After just a few minutes of equal breathing, you'll begin to feel more relaxed and in control as you're switching into the para-sympathetic system. As you start to feel more comfortable, you may gradually lengthen the breaths to a five count if you would like. The longer you continue the process, the more relaxed you'll feel, and the easier it will be to expand the count.

Again, what if the mind wanders? That's OK. Just refocus on your breathing. It's very normal for the mind to wander with this technique. Just keep refocusing back on the breath and the count.

Let's take the first step and give it a try. Are you ready to practice the stressbuster? You'll love this!

Put your cell phone on silent. Get into a comfortable position where you'll not be disturbed. Take a moment to focus on the position of your body. Notice where your body meets the chair, couch, or bed. Imagine the body gently sinking into that position. You can either close your eyes or leave them open. Please put all your focus on your breath now. Take a deep breath through your nose, completely filling up your lungs, hold it, hold it, now take a second breath and suck in more air through your nose, hold for a few seconds, and *slowly let it out* through your nose, emptying your lungs.

Now we begin with the *four count* as you breathe in through your nose, using your diaphragm, and feel the air go into your abdomen. Actually notice the feeling of the air as it travels through your nostrils. Yes, pay close attention to the air as it passes through your nose. Gently release the breath to the count of four while emptying the air out of your chest and tummy—not too deep and not too shallow. Each breath feels full and complete. The inbreath calmly changes to the outbreath. The inbreath lingers for just a moment before releasing, like a calm ocean wave pausing for just a moment before it changes direction and flows back out to sea. Continue now with this technique as you relax and feel the air flow in and flow out. Do this for a few minutes or so now, please.

How was that?

Ahh. And that was only a few minutes! You're learning to respond to stress instead of negatively reacting, which is very good. And, with practice, you'll be able to switch on your parasympathetic system whenever you would like. This technique is also known as belly breathing or mindful breathing meditation.

Taking control of your breath has been around for thousands of years. Obviously, this stressbuster is your very basic beginner-level technique. Entire books have been written on breathing meditations, such as mindfulness breathing, meditations with varying breathing counts, using one nostril at a time, taking a second to pause between breaths, using your mouth only, laying down, burning candles, lighting incense, and so on. They all arrive at the parasympathetic nervous system.

One book I would highly recommend is *Breath* by James Nestor.

FOR HOW LONG SHOULD I
DO THE TECHNIQUE?

You can spend a few minutes or an entire breathing meditation for ten to twenty-five minutes or even more. I love doing a twenty-minute mindful breathing meditation. It will really clear your mind and reboot your system. Again, the key is to place your entire focus on your breath. If any other thoughts come into your mind, gently let them go and refocus your attention on the breathing.

Please make it a goal to practice the stressbuster breathing technique. Start with just *five minutes* a day for the next few weeks; you can do that. You may want to set a timer before you begin. Experiment with it. Play with it. Have fun. Some people like to expand the breath to a count of five, six, or higher. You may enjoy it so much you find yourself doing it for ten minutes a day or more. Do what feels comfortable—but do it, because this also brings your focus into the present moment.

Remember: your greatest power to choose is always in the present moment.

As a reminder, if you do feel stressed out every day, then you absolutely must change the pattern for optimal health. Sometimes the underlying stress is out of your conscious awareness, resulting in you routinely not feeling comfortable or relaxed. As stated previously, continual day-after-day stress is very hurtful on many levels.

Making mental adjustments by parking your nervous system in the parasympathetic gear is a great skill and quite an accomplishment. As you'll see, it enhances your personal power and yields overall health benefits. Mark my words: learning and practicing this breathing meditation technique will create a positive ripple effect that will touch unexpected areas of your life. That's why I'm suggesting you start doing the breathing meditation every day. Start with five minutes a day. As a reminder to yourself, you may want to write a Post-it that says, "I practice parasympathetic breathing every day." Put it up on your bathroom mirror.

Wait, isn't that advertising to yourself?

Yes, it is! And it costs significantly less than a Super Bowl ad!

One of the advantages and benefits of this book is that as you apply the tips and techniques within, you'll soon discover yourself feeling less stressed and more relaxed in all areas of your life. Why? Because you'll gradually see and experience feeling in more control of your greatest power. You'll begin to say no to anxiety, fear, and racing thoughts, and you'll say yes to handling yourself with the ease and confidence that you naturally deserve. Therefore, you may notice how enjoying life is your new daily routine.

Again, I highly recommend James Nestor's book, *Breath*.

And now, coming up next is chapter five, where you'll be hypnotized! You may have already heard about hypnosis, and I'm sure you're excited to learn more. Lock the doors, dim the lights, turn off your cell phone, and follow my words to the next page.

CHAPTER 5

YOU'LL BE HYPNOTIZED! (OR WHAT'S HYPNOSIS?)

EVERY DAY, IN EVERY WAY, I'M GETTING BETTER AND BETTER.
—EMILE COUE

THE REMAINING CHAPTERS ARE STEP number three in your process toward a *Powerful Mindset of Health, Happiness, and Success.*

In this exciting chapter, you'll be learning:

- All hypnosis is self-hypnosis
- How hypnosis works and the falsehoods of hypnosis
- How you experience self-hypnosis practically every day
- Your three minds (you thought you only had one!): the conscious, subconscious, and unconscious
- Why a focused mental state is needed for successful hypnosis
- The critical factor of the conscious mind
- Being hypnotized using auto-suggestion
- How hypnosis and neurons team up to create new, positive thoughts

It's OK if you're not initially familiar with some of the concepts. As you read, they'll become clear. Be ready to learn new things about yourself as you work with proven techniques for successful change. This will be a very positive and eye-opening read, and perhaps positively life-changing.

At one time in my life, I would *never* be alone in a room with a hypnotist. I saw movies with hypnotists controlling people's minds, and I thought they might be able to control my mind. I was ignorant of how hypnosis really works. In the addendum, I'll share the amazing full story of how I surprisingly became involved with this work.

My initial introduction to hypnosis was a seminar I attended in 1995 in New York City, called "Success with Self-Hypnosis." The instructor, Dr. Barry Seedman, an accomplished man in his early sixties, delivered a few main points. He said that anyone can be guided into a relaxed state of hypnosis if they want to do it. He demonstrated that *all hypnosis is self-hypnosis*. This means that you're always in charge of accepting a suggestion or not. If what's being said during a hypnosis session is something you would not choose to accept, then it will not go into your subconscious. No one else is controlling your mind.

Dr. Seedman also stated that the subconscious mind cannot tell the difference between a real or an imagined event. *ScienceDaily* confirmed this is a fact, and it was determined to be true through brain imaging studies. The same areas of the brain light up when someone is imagining a real or a perceived threat.

Three main points to consider so far:

- All hypnosis is self-hypnosis.
- The subconscious mind cannot tell the difference between a real or an imagined event.
- Anyone can be guided into a relaxed state of hypnosis if they would like to be.

WHAT, EXACTLY, IS HYPNOSIS?

In 1959, the American Medical Association and the American Psychological Association approved hypnosis as a therapeutic tool. Currently, the Mayo Clinic states, "Hypnosis, also referred to as hypnotherapy or hypnotic suggestion, is a trance-like state in which you have a heightened focus and concentration. Hypnosis is usually done with the help of a therapist using verbal repetition and mental images. In hypnosis, you usually feel calm and relaxed, and are more open to suggestions."

My definition is, "Hypnosis is a powerful tool that you can use to help you relax, change any habit, change any thought, or enhance any skill."

Even though hypnosis has become more mainstream, 90 percent of the people I meet have no real understanding about how the process works. After reading and working through this chapter, you'll be in the elite ten percent. And I'd like to add that understanding the hypnotic process will obviously enhance your experience.

Millions of people use hypnosis to improve their lives. Some notables you may be familiar with include Oprah, Ben Affleck, Drew Barrymore, Jessica Alba, Fergie, Lily Allen, Kevin Costner, Ashton Kutcher, and Eva Mendes. Ellen DeGeneres had her hypnotherapist as a guest on her show. During an appearance on *The Tonight Show*, actor Matt Damon revealed that using hypnosis was one of the best decisions of his entire life. You can see the video on my website, HappyHypnotist.com or YouTube: https://www.youtube.com/watch?v=242uxOoX4YM.

Numerous professional athletes have used or are currently using the tool of hypnosis and self-hypnosis to improve their performance. Some of the famous athletes on that list: golf champion Tiger Woods, boxer Mike Tyson, soccer legend David Beckham, baseball hall of famer Rod Carew, tennis great Jimmy Connors, PGA golfer Deana Rushworth, and Oakland Raiders NFL kicker Jeff Jaeger. All these people have benefited from hypnosis. And you're the next to benefit, because, later in this chapter, you'll experience a self-hypnosis exercise.

Before we continue, let's contrast the interventions of mainstream medicine, as practiced in the United States, versus seeing a hypnotherapist for the same issue. In conversations with family and friends, the consensus was that most physicians will write a prescription. See if you agree: Most doctors usually give pills for anxiety. True? If you want to stop smoking, be ready for nicotine pills or a nicotine patch. Correct? If you want to lose weight, you'll get a pill. Right? There are even pills now to help you remember which pills to take! (Just kidding on the last one, but it's coming).

In contrast, hypnotherapy and self-hypnosis are noninvasive, nonmedical approaches that tap into your own mind. The approaches utilize a focused mental state to communicate with your subconscious mind to create new responses, new thoughts, new attitudes, new behaviors, or new feelings. No pills are needed. I want to be clear that, yes, there are times you might need a prescription from your doctor. But when you can accomplish something without medication, why not?

SOME MISCONCEPTIONS ABOUT HYPNOSIS

Some common misconceptions about hypnosis include that hypnosis is a form of sleep and that you're "under the control" of the hypnotist.

The HistoryofHypnosis.org states that the word *hypnosis* was coined in 1841 by British surgeon and therapist James Braid. *Hypnos* is the Greek word that means *sleep*. It may appear like a form of sleep; however, it's *not* sleep at all. Again, it's simply a focused mental state.

Interestingly, *therapeia* is also a Greek word that means *curative* or *healing*. Therefore, the word *hypnotherapist* could be defined as *healing sleep* or *healing through hypnosis*.

Based on movies and TV, you might think you're under the control of the hypnotist, but that's not true. The fact is that *no one* can hypnotize you to do something against your will or your morals. This has been proven in the court of law in the United States. For instance, I could not hypnotize you to rob a bank and give me the money and forget it happened. Now, if you're a professional bank robber, and your thieving techniques have diminished, and you would like to improve them, hypnosis is a terrific tool for enhancing skills. (For the record, though, I would *not* choose to work with anyone whose goal is to break a law.)

Over the years I have helped many athletes enhance their skills, including a Boston Marathon runner, a professional baseball player, a jockey, golfers, and basketball and baseball players, all of who used hypnosis to improve their game. All professional sports teams have either hypnotherapists or mental coaches to work with the athletes to enhance their performance.

Have you ever seen a hypnosis stage show? It might appear that the hypnotist is controlling the participants. Occasionally, I host these events that are billed as comedy hypnosis shows. I simply ask for volunteers to come up on stage if they would like to experience hypnosis. They understand that they're participating in a comedy show, and they're willing to accept suggestions that will be turned into entertainment. However, these volunteers will not accept a suggestion that is against their morals or values. Here are some examples of the comedy show suggestions:

- The men are pregnant and ready to deliver a baby.
- Saying things like, "When I point to you and say, 'Sleep,' you instantly close your eyes and go into a deep sleep," or "Your tongue stopped working, so you can't talk clearly anymore."

When the participants follow the suggestions, the show becomes very entertaining and fun. Imagine seeing a big, strapping, two-hundred-pound man giving birth, with his legs spread out, doing Lamaze breathing exercises, as I'm directing him.

"The head is coming out. Push harder! Push harder!"

And he acts as if he is really giving birth. The audience is in stitches.

But what would happen if all the volunteers decided not to accept the suggestions? The entertainment would come to a quick stop. (And the hypnotist would hope that he remembered how to juggle chainsaws.) This part of the process is quite simple. It's up to the individual to accept a suggestion or not, whether it's a stage hypnosis show or clinical hypnotherapy session. As stated, all hypnosis is self-hypnosis.

What behavior would you like to change? Maybe you would like to stop smoking, control your food intake, or not feel anxious in social situations. Whatever it is, did you ever wonder why you can't simply tell yourself not to be that way, and it's done? Let's say you have a fear of mice. Even if you see a mouse on TV, you feel afraid. Why can't you just repeat to yourself, "I'm not afraid of mice anymore," and then the fear goes away? It simply does not work. Why?

There are a couple of reasons. First, whenever you want to accomplish something, it's very important that you frame it with positive behavior. Instead of saying, "I'm not afraid of mice," say it this way: "I feel calm and relaxed around mice." See the difference? (You'll read more about the importance of framing in Chapter Six.)

Repeating the phrase "I'm not afraid of mice" was also ineffective because it wasn't delivered to your subconscious mind, which is the home of the fear. If you had been able to get the correct message of change into your subconscious, it would have made all the difference.

Some questions:

- What's the difference between the conscious and subconscious mind?
- How exactly does hypnotic communication work?

- How is the subconscious programmed?

- Why do all definitions of hypnosis include phrases such as *trance-like state*, *heightened focus*, or *intense concentration*?

What exactly does intense concentration, heightened focus, or a trance-like state even mean? These terms simply mean you're mentally focused on something. It's a normal state of mind that we all experience. Though you may not realize it, you experience a hypnotic state or focused mental state every day. Let's look at some examples:

- When you're daydreaming or fantasizing about something, your mind is focused on your dream. It's as if you've blocked out other stimuli around you.

- When you're in your car and drive right past your exit because your mind was elsewhere, you're still in control and would have reacted if a car swerved toward you. Or if you're daydreaming and a fire alarm goes off, you'll still hear it. If you're in a hypnosis session and there is an emergency, you'll respond to it.

- Have you ever been watching TV, reading a book, or working on your computer when somebody calls your name, and you don't really hear the person because you're so focused on what you're doing? This is a focused mental state also known as the *hypnotic state*. (Many spouses and parents are familiar with this one!)

- Have you ever meditated? In the previous chapter, you had an introduction to a simple breathing meditation. Most meditators are simply calming and clearing their mind. Being in a meditative state, a hypnotic state, or a trance state are all simply focused mental states.

As stated previously, there are huge benefits for taking the time to relax and be in a focused mental state—meditation. Meditation is a great way to stop your mind from incessant thinking. It's good to hit your pause button occasionally.

CONSCIOUS, SUBCONSCIOUS, AND UNCONSCIOUS MIND

Did you know you have *three* minds? You have a conscious mind, a subconscious mind, and an unconscious mind. What part of your mind runs your immune system, your eyes blinking, your heart beating, and other involuntary functions? That would be your *unconscious mind*. We don't really deal with the unconscious mind in hypnosis, so let's just put that aside for now. We have two minds left to discuss: the conscious and subconscious.

Now that you understand what the *focused mental state* means, let's discuss the conscious, the subconscious, and the critical factor of the conscious mind. You'll see how these parts are connected in terms of how and why hypnosis works. After that, we will do a mini self-hypnosis session. This will be fun!

First, please answer this question: what did you have for dinner last night? Take a moment right now and think about that. When it comes into your mind, whatever it was—broiled Skittles, fried possum, sautéed squirrel—hang on to that answer, please, because we will come back to it.

What did you have for dinner yesterday? I'm asking because I want you to access your *conscious mind*. When you pull an answer from your short-term memory, you're accessing your conscious mind. Let's say you're driving your car very late at night, and you get a flat tire. Several thoughts come into your mind:

- Is this a safe place for me to pull over?
- Am I going to be able to change this tire by myself?
- Do I even have a spare tire?
- Should I call for help?

What you're doing in this instance is analyzing the situation. When you analyze, you're accessing your conscious mind. The conscious mind is also the home of your willpower. Think of willpower as a short burst to get you over a hump. When someone tries to stop smoking, the willpower they utilize may only last for a day or two. When someone who eats a lot of sweets says, "I'm going to stop it," they may be able to stop it for a short while. But after a couple of days, they're usually right back where they started. Willpower is a good mechanism for short-term goals, but it does not necessarily yield long-term gain.

To review, the conscious mind houses your short-term memory, analytical skills, willpower, and also provides explanations for your behavior—the reasons why you do the things you do. Ask, "Why am I reading this book right now?" You may be curious about hypnosis, or you have a specific habit you would like to change. Whatever your response, please understand that the answer came from your conscious mind.

What part of your mind controls your habits, your emotions, your permanent memory, and is home to your personal computer program? That, my friend, is your beautiful and mega-powerful *subconscious mind*. Hypnotherapists agree that the elements of your subconscious include your emotions, your habits, and your beliefs. Your subconscious mind is your program.

The main purpose of the subconscious is to act out the program. Let me repeat that: the job of your subconscious is to follow the instructions in your individual program. Think of it as the inner workings of your laptop or tablet, which, as you know, just follows the instructions in the computer program.

So, how do you change your subconscious program?

My hypnosis instructors taught us about a part of the mind called the *critical factor* of the conscious mind. Think of this critical factor as a guard that stands between the gateway of the conscious and subconscious. Imagine this guard analyzes everything you think and say about yourself. If what you say or think matches the programming in the subconscious mind, that idea or thought can enter. Like a hot knife through butter, the idea goes right in to the subconscious. If you say something that does not match the program, the guard rejects the idea. Now the idea is not permitted to enter the subconscious.

When you're in a focused mental state, the critical factor leaves the door to the subconscious wide open. Therefore, attaining a focused mental state is an important initial step. It opens the gateway that allows new thoughts, new images, and new behaviors into the subconscious.

The good news is that when new thoughts and ideas are allowed in, the subconscious *automatically* begins to create a new program. You read that correctly: when you communicate with your subconscious this way, your program begins to change. Why? The answer is simple—because this is how the subconscious mind functions. Like a compass always points north, or Newton's law of gravity (whatever goes up must come down), once you allow suggestions into the subconscious, it automatically starts imprinting the new information. This is the powerful truth of the way it works.

I'd like you to realize your subconscious mind is like a ten-year-old child who accepts everything literally. Imagine you're talking to a ten-year-old who believes that everything you're saying is 100 percent true.

As stated earlier, your subconscious cannot tell the difference between a real or an imagined event. Think about that. When you're programming positive images into your subconscious, it thinks they're real! Let's say you've a bad habit of smoking, and you want to stop. You infuse your subconscious with images of *I'm a nonsmoker, I'm smoke-free, I say no to cancer sticks*, and the mind views the images as real. Obviously, this is the main reason why hypnosis is so successful because it begins to help you rewrite the program.

Again, I'd like to highlight the difference between meditation and hypnosis. When you meditate, you're in the moment, enjoy the relaxing feeling, focus on your breathing, embrace calmness, and clear your mind. In hypnosis, once you arrive at the relaxing feeling of calm, then you communicate the changes you would like to enter into the subconscious. Meditation is more of a passive activity, whereas hypnosis is a more active one. Do you see the difference? As noted, hypnosis is a tool to reach your subconscious mind. I'd like to elaborate on this topic.

What tools have you used around your home? Have you ever needed a tool for a project? Let's say you want to hang a big, beautiful piece of artwork in your living room. You'll need some tools—items like picture hooks, nails, a hammer, and a level. After you've completed the task, the picture is up on the wall, and it looks great. It hangs exactly as you had imagined. You feel happy. When someone asks, "Who hung that picture?" you would naturally respond, "I did!" You're not going to say that the tools did. My point is that *hypnosis is a tool.* It does not do the job for you. It just makes it easier for you to accomplish your goal.

To review: your habits, also known as your *program*, are in your subconscious. To access the subconscious, you need to get into a focused mental state, or the *hypnotic state*, and deliver the changes to update the program. I must add that it's easy and fun; and as you'll see, it's obviously very helpful to those who follow through with the process.

LET'S EXPERIENCE SELF-HYPNOSIS

This session will focus on relaxation and the feeling of calm, something from which most of us can all benefit. Many doctors say that too much stress can cause illness. On the other hand, taking time to relax has been scientifically proven to have major physical and emotional benefits. This fact was verified by Harvard graduate Dr. Herbert Benson in his book *The Relaxation Response* (1975).

Normally, when I do self-hypnosis, I turn on a self-hypnosis audio file, lie back, relax, and listen for about twenty minutes or so. Since you're reading instead of listening to an audio file, we can use *auto-suggestion self-hypnosis*. The first step will be to attain a focused mental state. Then, you'll repeat a short statement, also known as a *mantra*, to your subconscious.

This mini session will give you a small taste, a tiny sip, of what self-hypnosis feels like by just reading the next few pages. Obviously, this will not be the same as a full-blown guided session, but it will be a good introduction.

It may seem funny to say this when you're reading a book, but you'll need to be in a place where you'll not be disturbed, because your eyes will be closed at one point. Our focus will be on relaxation and calmness. Remember: being in a focused mental state is a normal state of mind. This experience will give you a *little idea* of how the process feels. I will explain the technique and then repeat the instructions a couple times. Then it will be your turn to experience self-hypnosis.

The name of this mini self-hypnosis session I created is "Five Feels Good." It is also known as the stairway of relaxation. This drill will take you down an imaginary short flight of five steps, where each step brings you into a deeper state of relaxation. When you reach the bottom of the steps, you'll imagine yourself feeling very relaxed, and then repeat a mantra to yourself five times—*I'm relaxed, and I feel good; I'm relaxed, and I feel good; I'm relaxed, and I feel good; I'm relaxed, and I feel good; I'm relaxed, and I feel good.* Then just enjoy the feeling of calm. That's it.

Clients have reported that, after this small sample of self-hypnosis, their shoulder and neck muscles felt more relaxed afterward. Others have said they felt very calm and peaceful during this short exercise. I think you'll enjoy it. Again, the instructions will be repeated a couple times. Let's begin.

I CALL THIS EXERCISE "FIVE FEELS GOOD" IT IS ALSO KNOWN AS, "THE STAIRWAY OF RELAXATION"

First, read these instructions, then you will close your eyes and do the exercise.

You'll need to be in a place where you'll not be disturbed because your eyes will be closed. Silence or shut off your cell phone or other devices. Great—now we can begin.

In a short while, I will ask you to take a breath in as deep as you can and hold it, and then take a second breath, filling up your lungs to the max. Hold for a few seconds, and as you exhale through your nose, allow your eyes to close. Imagine you're standing on a short stairway of relaxation with just five steps to the bottom, they may even be numbered from five to one.

With each breath, you will envision yourself slowly walking down one step at a time as you count down from five to one. Each number brings you to the next step and into a deeper state of relaxation. By the time you reach the bottom of the stairs, expect that you will feel more relaxed. You will be in a light, focused mental state; then you repeat the mantra five times "I'm relaxed, and I feel good."

Do it like this, with each count you will inhale, and, on your exhale, say the number and the words, "feeling more relaxed" as you step down. You can say it out loud if you wish or silently to yourself. As you proceed down the steps, you enter into deeper states of relaxation.

You can pretend you feel your foot touch each step as you slowly count down from five to one. You may use your fingers to assist in your counting down if you wish.

It's ok if you do not initially grasp all the details here, with some practice you will be great at this.

See yourself at the top of the short stairway, take a slow deep breath and say "five," step down, say, "feeling more relaxed" on your exhale. Continue, take a slow deep breath and say "four" step down, say, "feeling more relaxed" on your exhale. Continue, take a slow deep breath and say "three" step down, say, "feeling more relaxed" on your exhale. Continue, take a slow deep breath and say "two" step down, say, "feeling more relaxed" on your exhale. Continue, take a slow deep breath and say "one" step down, say, "feeling more relaxed" on your exhale. Now slowly repeat the mantra five times

"I'm relaxed, and I feel good."

"I'm relaxed, and I feel good."

"I'm relaxed, and I feel good."

"I'm relaxed, and I feel good."

"I'm relaxed, and I feel good."

Allow your eyes to stay closed and focus on the calm feeling for a few moments. Then, whenever you feel ready, simply allow your eyes to open. You may notice the calming effect of this stairway relaxation exercise. This mini self-hypnosis session is a wonderful introduction for you.

Read these instructions one more time. Then it will be your turn.

Imagine your eyes are starting to feel heavy, sleepy, and re-laxed—heavy, sleepy, and relaxed. Take a big deep breath, and then take that second breath, and when you exhale, close your eyes. Imagine you're at the top of the stairway of relaxation with five steps down.

You will count down slowly from five to one; on the exhale, you will step down say the number and the words, "feeling more relaxed." Imagine that each number and each exhale takes you down one step. If you wish, you may also use the numbers five thousand, four thousand, three thousand, two thousand, and one thousand. These numbers may help you go slower, which is the pace we want. It's OK to use your fingers as you count down.

As you work your way down the five steps, you may imagine feeling your feet actually touching each step. Each number you say will make you feel more and more relaxed, as if each number is bringing you to a deeper level of relaxation. After you reach the last step and say the number one, you slowly repeat to yourself five times:

"I'm relaxed, and I feel good."

"I'm relaxed, and I feel good."

"I'm relaxed, and I feel good."

"I'm relaxed, and I feel good."

"I'm relaxed, and I feel good."

Then, just pause and enjoy the calm feeling of this mini self-hypnosis session. (Since you're repeating the mantra five times, some people have used their fingers to keep track). Whenever you feel ready, take a deep breath and open your eyes.

NOW IT'S REALLY TIME TO DO THIS

Since you just read this a couple of times, I bet you may have noticed some relaxed feelings. OK, let's go. It's time for you to do it on your own.

Take a big, deep breath and—you know by now—a second inhale to fill every bit of your lungs. Exhale slowly through your nose, close your eyes, and then imagine yourself at the top of the steps and start the countdown process…

Go, and enjoy!

Ahh, was that nice or what? It may have taken you a minute or so to complete this. Did you notice any relaxed feelings? Congratulations! You just experienced being hypnotized through self-hypnosis! This is just barely scratching the surface of feeling calm. (In my one-on-one sessions, depending on the client, we may take up to 20 minutes just breathing and relaxing to arrive at a deep hypnotic state). This drill is known as *auto-suggestion self-hypnosis*. The mantra you repeated can simply be changed to whatever you wish to work on. Let's say you are working on feeling more confident, your mantra may be, "I now feel relaxed and confident."

This is awesome! You're learning a new skill that will help you for the rest of your life. Obviously, the more you practice self-hypnosis, the easier and more proficient you'll become. Soon, you'll easily find yourself with the ability to feel totally relaxed in only minutes. In the next chapter, we'll get into more detail about successful self-hypnosis.

HOW WAS YOUR SUBCONSCIOUS INITIALLY PROGRAMMED?

Let's take a couple of minutes to reflect on how your subconscious mind was initially programmed. When you're young, the subconscious is an open vessel that is easily programmed and accepts everything as reality. Your early childhood experiences created impressions in your subconscious. Your beliefs, your personality, and your program are the result of how you perceived, interpreted, and internalized experiences. By the time you reach your mid-teens, your basic program is established, and by the late teens and early twenties, your adult program is pretty much locked in. But always remember that tapping into your subconscious with hypnosis is the key to open the lock.

When someone's early years contain negative thoughts, negative fears, or feelings of insecurity, their program is often riddled with anxiety, sadness, and depression. These experiences in childhood may also create emotional blocks as adults. The opposite is true as well. If the early program is filled with loving, positive, and joyful emotions, this usually brings about a happy and positive person. It makes sense, right?

It's important to note that all your experiences are subjective. Early childhood is no different. I've seen how one sibling hated their childhood, and the other thought it was a good childhood. One person may hate if it's raining, and another person may love the rain. All your experiences boil down to how you personally interpreted them at the time.

Dr. Seedman told us about a client who was sexually abused by her father. The next client he saw that day complained that her father was the worst person and ruined her emotionally.

He asked, "Why do you say that?"

She said, "My father made me stand in the corner of the room and stare at the wall if I didn't listen to him."

It all goes back to how we internalize and personalize events. That will determine what your program will reflect. Again, I want to state that I've seen my clients overcome, let go of, and move on from serious emotional abuse with hypnosis.

Using self-hypnosis to funnel new, positive information into the powerful subconscious mind is your ticket to a new and improved program. This reprogramming process can neutralize negative emotions and wash them out of the subconscious. It can be done with amazing speed. One of the big reasons why my heart loves this work is because I have seen repeatedly how a couple of clinical hypnosis sessions can clear decades of anxiety out of the subconscious. Hypnosis allows the client to be free of damaging past emotional issues and to move forward in a happy and positive way. You'll see more about this in chapter eleven, with "Successful Subconscious Case Studies."

HOW DOES HYPNOSIS CHANGE YOUR THOUGHTS?

When you communicate with your subconscious mind, you're changing the actual construction of your thoughts and creating new thoughts. Let me explain. If you could take a magical micro-scope to peek inside your brain, you would see neurotransmitters and neurons flying around. Neurons are informational mes-sengers, the basic building blocks of the nervous system. These neurons contain the information for each thought. According to the journal *Nature*, we have about eighty-six billion nerve cells in the brain and many more neuroglia (or glial cells) that support the neurons. That's *billions* with a B! It's a challenge to really comprehend how big the number one billion is. One billion is such a huge number; if you were to just stand still and count to one billion, it would take you about twenty-nine years!

I was taught to think of each individual thought as a hologram. What's a hologram? A hologram is a three-dimensional unit that is all-encompassing, in that any single piece of a hologram contains the *same information* as the other pieces. If you were to cut a neuron (or thought) into two unequal pieces, each piece still contains the same exact information. It's as if each piece still contains the same DNA code. When you add new information to a nerve cell (or thought) via hypnosis, it's as if the entire DNA of that nerve cell changes. *Bingo!* That nerve cell has been altered and so has the entire hologram and program. Do you understand what this means? If you have a real negative emotional thought that is bringing on sad or unpleasant feelings, once we introduce new information via hypnosis to that specific thought, it is impossible for the thought to affect you in a negative way again because it has been permanently changed!

New thoughts equal new additions to the nerve cell, which result in a permanent change in feelings and behavior. You could say that hypnosis reconstructs you at the level of your nerve cells, creating new thoughts and feelings that result in positive improvements to your program and behaviors. Is that amazingly beautiful and simple or what? Yes, it is! And it helps people move on from negative past experiences.

To review: the hypnotic state is a normal state of mind that you can use as a tool to communicate with the subconscious mind to change any behavior, redirect any thought, or enhance any quality. No pills are needed. All hypnosis is self-hypnosis.

Kudos to you. You now know a method of self-hypnosis—the auto-suggestion method. Let's continue the adventure into your mind with the importance of framing and tips for success with self-hypnosis. You're getting veerrry sleeeepy…

Kidding.

Next page, please.

CHAPTER 6

SUCCESS WITH SELF-HYPNOSIS AND THE IMPORTANCE OF POSITIVE FRAMING

THOSE WHO ACHIEVE MAKE MISTAKES, BUT NEVER MAKE THE BIGGEST MISTAKE OF ALL—DOING NOTHING!
—ATTRIBUTED TO BENJAMIN FRANKLIN

I LOVE BEN FRANKLIN'S QUOTE. And the fact that *you're now doing something* by learning the keys to self-hypnosis is outstanding! The information in this chapter is vital for your long-term success. Let me say that again, please. The information you're about to consume is *essential for your success.*

Our lesson is going to include:

- Two types of self-hypnosis.
- Importance of positive framing; and
- Tips for success with self-hypnosis.

Self-hypnosis is a process that results in, first and foremost, attaining the hypnotic state, which is a meditative state of mind that delivers instructions through auto-suggestion *or* through audio to the subconscious. The subsequent chapters will introduce more techniques used to rewrite the subconscious, including a visit to a professional hypnosis office that's followed by subconscious success stories. By reading these chapters sequentially, you'll be 100 percent prepared for your self-hypnosis scripts at the end of the book.

If self-hypnosis is a new skill for you, remember that you'll improve with practice. If I handed you a ball and said to throw it at a target, initially, you most likely would miss the mark. But with practice, you would zero in and hit the target. You'll find that your self-hypnosis skills also improve quickly.

SELF-HYPNOSIS AUTO-SUGGESTION

The mini self-hypnosis session you experienced in the previous chapter is a good first step. As you continue to work with self-hypnosis, feel free to experiment. You could choose to count down ten steps or any other number. Play with it. You can repeat your mantra ten times, twenty times, or whatever feels right to you. One obvious strength of auto-suggestion is that you don't need anything except yourself to perform the task. Once you're familiar with the process, inserting a new mantra or goal statement is a breeze.

AUDIO SELF-HYPNOSIS

Have you ever heard of using a guided meditation specifically to relax or go to sleep? This is also where you relax and listen to an audio recording. It's really the same as self-hypnosis, without using the word *self-hypnosis.*

Using headphones or earbuds while listening is recommended. The beginning of the audio is a guided relaxation into the focused mental state. As you relax and listen, the information is delivered to your subconscious. That's it—you're done. Was that easy or what? As you now know, once your subconscious receives the information, it begins to reprogram. Hallelujah!

With self-hypnosis, repetition is the key to success. Let me say that again: repetition of self-hypnosis is the key to achieving your goal. Do it every day, every other day, twice a day, or three times a day if you wish. Keep working with it until you reach your goal. It's only a matter of time—you'll be successful!

Auto-suggestion and audio self-hypnosis are both great tools. Which one should you use? Initially, I'd suggest using both. As you continue to experience the process, you may prefer one tool over the other.

Here are some success tips and pointers on making your own recordings. The first question for you: When will you be listening to this? Do you want to create something you can use during the day, when you can rest and relax for about 20 minutes, or would you like to work on helping yourself drift into a good night's sleep? The choice is yours.

Most of these suggestions are also perfect for adjusting your mindset in daily life. Every step is covered, from how to specifically word your suggestions, tenses, goals, believability, tone of speech, and so on. These tips will also train your brain to think in a positive way, which is a good thing!

HERE ARE YOUR TOP TWELVE TIPS FOR MAKING A SELF-HYPNOSIS SCRIPT

1. Have a Specific Goal

It's essential to have a specific goal in mind for your self-hypnosis. In life, the same rule applies. What is it you would like to accomplish? Get a good night's sleep? Create a new healthy habit? Would you like to relax for 20 minutes and reboot with some positive suggestions?

Imagine you're on a boat in the middle of the ocean, and you have no navigational equipment—no GPS or compass. You're lost. That's the effect of not having a goal. You are just drifting.

You may have multiple goals, such as eating healthier, exercising, weight control, not feeling anxious, or better sleep, and so on. To begin your self-hypnosis journey, let's focus on one goal at a time. If you do have multiple goals, select the one you believe will be the easiest for you. Once you see success in one area, then move on to the next goal.

Many people would simply like to feel more confident, so I included some suggestions for confidence in all the self-hypnosis scripts. Sometimes we might feel like we're stuck, or we just don't know what to do. One of your self-hypnosis scripts I've included is called "Your Inner Adviser," which is very helpful for this situation.

2. Frame Your Language Positively

When creating your goal statement and various suggestions, negative phrasing can cause mental blocks and impede your progress. In day-to-day life, the same rule applies. It's fundamental that you understand that the subconscious is blind to the word *not*. For instance, if I say, "Don't think of a red blinking traffic light. Don't picture a red blinking traffic light." Does a red blinking traffic light come into your mind?

How about when I say, "Don't let the whirling sound of a loud siren come into your mind. Don't think of what a loud siren sounds like when you hear it." Did you hear the loud siren sound even though I said "don't"?

To get the best results while practicing self-hypnosis, you must state the specific behavior or action you would like to achieve. To get the best results while practicing self-hypnosis, you must state the specific behavior or action you would like to achieve. (Yep, I said it twice)

This is a very good rule to follow with your everyday self-talk. Why? Repeat after me: Your mind goes in the d_ _ _ _ _ _ _ _ o_ y_ _ _ t_ _ _ _ _ _ _.

Did you fill in the blanks?

As a parent, I took this positive framing concept to heart. The rule is simple: let your children know what specific behavior you expect, not what behavior you don't want. Let's say two young kids are having a spat. It's not effective to say, "Stop fighting."

Why? Because the word *fighting* is still there. Instead, say, "Play nicely together. Get along with each other. You're on the same team. Be good teammates."

If you would like your child to get their shoes off the couch, it won't be optimal to say, "Don't put your shoes on the couch." Why? Because "shoes on the couch" is still in the request. Instead, say, "Please keep your shoes off of the couch. A couch is what you sit on."

If your toddler grabs something they're not supposed to play with, say, "Please put that back and play with one of your toys." Or say, "Put that down, please, and play with one of your toys."

If a child whines constantly, never say, "Stop whining!" because you're using the word *whine* in the goal. You can say, "Stop acting like that." Alternatively, ask them to, "Please use your words, and tell me how I can help." Or say, "Please act like a calm child. Everything is OK."

Notice when they're acting like a calm child and point it out.

"I like how you're acting now. That's good behavior."

See what I mean? You're reinforcing the positive behavior. Always give them a goal by stating the specific action or behavior you want. This rule always applies in self-hypnosis as well. Remember when I said the subconscious mind is like a ten-year-old? It takes everything literally.

Here's a memory from my childhood. I was seven years old and moping around one day, and my mom asked, "What's the matter?"

I said, "I'm bored."

Raising her voice, she said, "What? No one acts like that here. Go outside and play."

She gave me a specific direction. That was the last time I felt bored. Thanks, Mom!

In his book, *The Psychology of Winning*, Denis Waitley tells the following baseball story to illustrate the importance of giving exact directions: It was the bottom of the ninth inning with the game on the line. The coach came out of the dugout to give instructions to the pitcher. The coach said only ten words to the pitcher and then returned to the dugout.

The coach said, "Don't give this batter a low and outside pitch."

Naturally, the pitcher heard "low and outside," so that's exactly where his next pitch went. The hitter connected with a line drive for a game-winning double.

As you can probably guess, the coach should have said, "Keep the pitch on the inside of the plate."

Here's how I helped my children focus on getting good grades using this concept. From middle school through high school, I offered each child ten dollars for every A they received on their report cards, but I told them that any C would cancel an A. This was in the nineties, so if you would like to use this for your children, you may want to increase the amount. Along the same lines, I gave them goals by encouraging them to always do their best, work to be the smartest in their class, and participate in class discussions.

I also created individual self-hypnosis sleep audios for my children to listen to as they fell asleep. These scripts were, most of all, calming and relaxing to guide them into a pleasant, safe night's sleep. Sometimes children need to unwind so they can get a good night's sleep.

The audio calmly peppered them with "You feel sleepy, your eyes are sleepy, you feel safe and comfortable," and so on. And then, my children heard positive suggestions, such as: "Your parents love you, your family loves you, listen to your parents, listen to your teachers, do your best, participate in class discussions, you enjoy school, you love learning new things, you're a nice person, you respect everyone, you enjoy being helpful."

And there was my favorite—"...you have the greatest dad" (kidding on that one).

These self-hypnosis audios worked well for my three children. One became an Emmy-nominated TV producer. One is an entrepreneur and CEO of his own investment advisory company, (www.Retire.us) that has over fifty employees. And one has a master's degree in engineering and is currently working on the technology for self-driving cars. It warms my heart that my children are happy, independent, and successful. (Yes, I offer a selection of these recordings, entitled *Self-Hypnosis Audios for Children*, available at my Positive Store at www.HappyHypnotist.com.)

Let me give you another example of choosing the correct framing. Imagine you have anger issues and frequently blow up and yell at people. You decide this behavior is not serving you, so you want to change it. When you make a self-hypnosis recording, obviously you'll *not* say, "I will stop yelling and losing my temper."

Frame it in terms of the positive behavior you want to achieve. Say, "I control my reactions in a calm way. I focus on improving my communication skills in a friendly and positive way. I see myself talking with others, and no matter what they say or do, I remain calm and positive. People are noticing how calm and positive I am now."

3. Know Your Intention

What's your purpose? What's your ambition? Your intention underpins all of your behavior. Most of the time we might not be consciously aware of our intention. Reading this will help you understand the importance of knowing what your purpose is.

Let's use another boat analogy. Imagine you're on a sailboat and there's no wind. You're just sitting very still on the water. When the wind picks up, you can move! Think of the wind as your intention that will propel you. Your intention can be like the wind for your sails.

Is your intention positive or negative? Always consider the intention behind your goal. Let's say your goal is to graduate nursing school. Your intention is to provide a future for yourself as you help others. You receive enjoyment and personal fulfillment in this positive work.

Zeroing in on the intention and understanding what's behind any goal will help you succeed. What if your goal is to have an improved relationship with someone? You may want to frame your intentions as: *Do I want to be helpful? Do I want to be considerate? Do I want to be more affectionate? Do I want to listen better?* Maybe all of them will work for you.

Understanding your intentions will positively benefit you and your success! Some of my daily intentions include to be loving, kind, funny, and friendly. It's OK if we don't agree on something. Yes, it's OK if we have different opinions. Plus, I intend to have fun today!

4. Be Specific

Regardless of your focus, drill in on the details. For example, I will start my exercise routine Monday, Wednesday, and Friday at 3:00 p.m. I will start my homework thirty minutes after I get home from school. I will listen to my self-hypnosis recording for twenty minutes a day when I wake up at seven in the morning.

You may want to write down some specifics of your goal.

5. Make Your Goals Believable and Realistic

Is your goal statement to *Be the supreme leader of planet Earth in twenty-one days?* You may want to give that goal statement a bit more time. Try goals like the following, and edit them to be specific to you:

- To see myself acting calmly at work;
- To see myself acting calmly in traffic;

- To be easygoing and enjoy socializing anywhere;
- To be smoke-free in (X) days;
- To be (X) pounds closer to my goal weight of (X) lbs. within (X) month(s);
- To increase my free-throw shooting percentage by (X) percent in (X) month(s).

When you get a chance write down some goals for yourself.

6. Be Repetitive

In your self-hypnosis, repeat your goal by stating it over and over. Reinforce what you want by stating your goal in a variety of ways. Let's say you want to master self-hypnosis, and you want to own the skill of being able to put yourself in a relaxed focused mental state. The following statements may be read five times, ten times, or even more in your session.

You could use all these statements or select only a few:

- I'm enjoying my self-hypnosis sessions.
- I feel a sense of accomplishment every time I do self-hypnosis.
- I see the benefits of using self-hypnosis.
- I see myself easily gliding into the hypnotic state to receive my positive statements.
- I feel my confidence growing stronger and stronger with my self-hypnosis skills.
- I envision myself taking time to relax and enjoy the hypnotic state.
- I'm now committed to mastering self-hypnosis.
- I see myself a year from now still using and benefiting from self-hypnosis.

- My greatest power is my power to choose, and I choose to master the skill of self-hypnosis.

- People know I'm a pro at self-hypnosis.

7. Emphasize the Reward of the Good Feelings You'll Have, Using Your Imagination

During your self-hypnosis session, envision the experience of happy, positive feelings as if you've already achieved your goal. State how happy and positive you feel now that you've achieved your goal. State how others notice that you feel happy and positive. Let's say your goal is to make an elite travel baseball team. Try the following:

- I see a big smile on my face when I'm selected.

- My parents and family are happy I was selected.

- I can hear my dad's voice saying, "Congratulations! All your hard work paid off."

- I look fit and trim in the new travel baseball uniform.

- I love how the new baseball uniform feels on my body, and I'm a happy person.

- I envision myself standing on the pitcher's mound, getting the sign from the catcher, and throwing my fastball right by a whiffing batter.

- I love my teammates, and our team picture looks great.

- I see myself celebrating another win.

Come up with some good feelings for one of your goals and write them down.

8. Use Tenses Effectively *

Here's the formula for using verb tenses: present tense, future tense, present tense. At the beginning of your recording, say everything using the present tense. Toward the end, switch to future-tense suggestions, and then end in the present tense. Below are some examples you could use in a script to help with weight control.

Start with present-tense suggestions:

- I'm eating less now.
- I'm eating more slowly now.
- I'm now a healthy consumer of food.
- I avoid unhealthy foods that contain sugar.
- Sugar is poison. I say "no" to poison.
- I know what's healthy for me, and I eat healthy foods.
- I'm eating less and enjoying it more.
- My stomach is now shrinking as I make healthy choices.
- I can say "no" to food any time I choose.
- I hear myself say, "I'm in control of food," and I mean it.
- It feels good to be in control of my food intake.

Future-tense suggestions might be:

- I can control my food intake tomorrow and always.
- I see myself in control of my food intake next week.
- When I see myself controlling my food intake, I feel confident and positive.
- When I'm on vacation next week, I will be eating slowly, eating less, and enjoying the food more.
- Wherever I may be in the future, I'm always in control of my food intake.
- I see my clothes fitting more comfortably.
- I see myself at the wedding looking and feeling fabulous.

You could end your session with:

- I'm now in control of what food goes in my mouth.

- I enjoy controlling my food intake.
- I eat less and enjoy the food more.
- I love controlling my food intake.
- I'm committed to staying healthy and fit.
- It's nice when I hear people say, "You look great."

* It's vital to imagine yourself being successful in the future. Most people are so busy living in the past that they never really plan for how they might perceive themselves in the days, weeks, months, and years ahead. Whatever it is you want to accomplish, take time every day to visualize yourself being happy and successful in the future, as if you've already achieved your goal.

9. Create an Effective Recording

Chapter 12 provides the self-hypnosis scripts. Complete the remaining chapters first, because they'll help you with more ideas and techniques to use for your success. When you speak the script into your recording device, remember to use a nice, relaxing, calm voice with a gentle, slow pace. Monotone is perfect for this work.

For optimal playback sound, you'll need to experiment with the distance between your mouth and the recording microphone. If your mouth is too close, you might get some distortion or pop sounds. You might want some relaxing music playing in the background. If you do, use music that gives you that calm feeling.

10. Determine the Length of the Recording

How long should a session be? Twenty to thirty minutes is the average for a session, but you can experiment. I've done audio sessions as short as ten minutes and as long as forty-five minutes. The exception may be when you're creating sleep or bedtime sessions. The sessions can be one hour in length. I would not go much over an hour in length for a sleep recording, because an audio is not something that should be played all night. SleepFoundation.org confirms that your brain prefers silence when it's in total sleep mode.

11. End the Recording

There's a generic way of closing a session, and there are a couple of other options we will discuss. Self-hypnosis recordings are usually delivered in a relaxed tone. However, when you wrap it up or close a session, coming back to conscious awareness, pick up your voice and add some energy to it. Start talking faster and louder, as long as it's not a specific sleep recording.

For example, "In a moment, your session will be ending. You'll hear me count from one to five, and by the time we reach the number five, you'll be alert and feeling great, like you just had the best nap you've had in a long time. You'll remember all of the positive suggestions."

Now put some energy into these statements.

"I'm going to count to the number five now, and when we reach five, you'll be wide awake and alert. One, starting to come up. Two, coming up more and more. Three, let some energy come into your body, feeling free to move and stretch. Four, eyes open. Five, wide awake and alert. Feeling great, wide awake and alert."

If you're making a specific sleep audio, then it will be peppered with, "You're drifting into a safe night's sleep. You'll sleep so deeply and so completely that, when you wake up, you'll feel refreshed and ready to go."

For a sleep audio, I would suggest you also start talking very softly with less volume toward the end. Use less volume with each of the last sentences. Your voice becomes quieter and quieter as you end the recording.

12. Listen to Your Recording

The next important decision to make—*when* will you listen to your recording? Create a goal and schedule specific time to enjoy self-hypnosis. Write the goal down!

SAMPLE: MY SELF-HYPNOSIS GOAL

I will set my alarm twenty minutes earlier each morning, at (enter the exact time and date), to listen to my self-hypnosis audio. I will do this for twenty-one consecutive days, and I will enjoy the process as it unfolds. Each week, I will assess my progress and adjust my goal if needed.

Within a short time, you'll feel the difference, and I guarantee you'll love it! Find a place where you'll not be disturbed. Put your cell phone on silent. Sit back or lie down and get as comfortable as you can without having your legs or ankles crossed. Good blood flow is important for self-hypnosis.

QUESTION: WHAT IF I FALL ASLEEP DURING MY SELF-HYPNOSIS SESSION?

It's OK if you fall asleep occasionally. Your mind will still hear the positive messages. And, as I've mentioned, if you have difficulty falling asleep at night, you may want to work on making a self-hypnosis sleep audio. I have included a "Get a Good Night's Sleep" script in back of the book. If you decide to make your own self-hypnosis sleep audio, I'd suggest not going over an hour in length. Once the mind goes into deep sleep, it's best to have silence.

More terrific tools and techniques to communicate with your subconscious are coming up next!

CHAPTER 7

TOOLS YOU NEED FOR
SUCCESSFUL PROGRAMMING

*IT'S ESSENTIAL TO HAVE GOOD TOOLS, AND
IT'S ALSO ESSENTIAL TO USE THE TOOLS
THE RIGHT WAY.*
—WALLACE D. WATTLES

THIS CHAPTER WILL INTRODUCE SOME awesome techniques (tools) that hypnotherapists employ to help reprogram the subconscious. The methods selected are perfect for audio self-hypnosis, so you can easily adapt the tools for your goals. Some of them can also be used as a stand-alone exercise, meaning no self-hypnosis is needed. But the methods are more powerful with self-hypnosis, as you'll see.

Are you ready for nine fabulous change methods? Here we go. Please consider how you may incorporate them into your own self-hypnosis work. Simply change or modify the words to fit your specific goal. As you work with these tools, you may notice how the information introduced earlier in the book (your greatest power and the two most important words) is being utilized.

Just reading these techniques will benefit you to a degree. But when you put them into your self-hypnosis session then *wow!* You'll really feel their power. Again, simply adapt and change any of the words below to fit your specific goal.

DIRECT SUGGESTION

What's *direct suggestion*? Military personnel follow direct commands from their superiors. Direct suggestion is exactly that: giving a direct order to the subconscious. For example, if your goal is to be confident about public speaking, the following direct suggestions are perfect:

- You enjoy your new ability of communicating in front of others.

- Any butterflies or other feelings you may experience before you give a speech you interpret as excitement and positivity toward getting your message out to the audience.

- You'll feel calm and confident in front of others. You're focused and feel confident as you look out and speak to the audience.

- You're a good public speaker.

- You enjoy having the audience's eyes focused on you as you deliver one of your speeches.

- You'll notice yourself feeling focused, confident, and happy in front of other people.

- You're a successful public speaker.

Let's say your goal is to feel confident while driving in traffic. The following direct suggestions are perfect:

- You're now a relaxed and confident driver in the city.

- You notice how calm you feel when driving your car. Whether there's traffic or not, you remain calm and focused behind the wheel.

- You see yourself easily handling city traffic with ease.

- As soon as you sit in your car, and you feel your body comfortably in the driver's seat, you say to yourself, "I'm a relaxed driver in traffic. I can do it."

- You enjoy driving in the city.

- Your friends and family notice what a relaxed, calm city driver you are.

- Put a Post-it on the dashboard of your car that reads "I stay relaxed and focused when I'm driving."

Below are more examples of direct suggestion, if your goal is to sleep better:

- You're now the type of person who falls asleep comfortably and easily.

- Once you get in bed, you enjoy the safe, comfortable feeling of lying down and saying "goodbye" to the day as you easily drift into a restful night's sleep.

- You realize your bed is your safe place to sleep.

- You go to bed the same time each night.

- You say "no" to any food three or four hours before sleep time.

- You practice excellent sleep hygiene, no screens a couple hours before bed, and you make it a priority to go outside in the morning to get fresh air and sunshine.

- You like the fact that you're now a good sleeper.

Direct suggestion is a powerful device to help you change.

MODELING

Modeling is using someone's image and likeness to learn how they perform. This technique has helped thousands of my clients over the years. You'll soon see that this is an amazing learning experience. Once you're *solidly in the hypnotic state*, this technique puts you in the shoes of the type of person you want to emulate. Modeling has you experience the world as someone who has already achieved what you want to improve on.

Step 1: Think of someone who you believe is great at whatever you would like to accomplish. This can be someone you know. It could be someone in the public eye. Let's say you would like more confidence in social situations. In your self-hypnosis session, you imagine a person who projects a lot of confidence in social situations. As you observe the person, notice they project tons of confidence. You observe how they enjoy themselves as they're with others.

Step 2: Now, envision yourself standing right next to them, shoulder to shoulder.

Step 3: As you envision standing shoulder to shoulder with that person, imagine magically merging your image into theirs—just blend the two. Now, imagine that you're looking out through their eyes and listening through their ears. In this way, you'll see the world as they do, and you'll feel their confidence. Enjoy the feeling.

Step 4: Slowly separate the images. As you emerge from the imagined scene, take the confident feelings with you. Realize that you *always had this confidence within you,* but you were not focusing on it. Now you know you have it. And it feels good!

"I AM" STATEMENTS

You now know the importance of "I am." Here are some powerful "I am" statements for public speaking:

- I am confident communicating in front of others.
- I feel confident and relaxed while speaking in front of others.
- I am focused and confident as I look out at the audience in front of me.
- I notice I feel focused, happy, and confident in front of other people.
- I am a successful public speaker.
- I enjoy being known as a successful public speaker.

Here are some terrific "I am" statements for feeling confident in social situations:

- I am noticing that I now feel comfortable, relaxed, and confident in social situations.
- I notice I feel relaxed and positive in front of other people.
- I am enjoying myself now when I'm with others.
- I like that I feel comfortable when socializing.
- I am the type of person who's interested in others.
- I am a good listener and people like that.
- I have fun when I socialize.
- I look for ways to laugh in social situations.

Here are some on-target "I am" statements for being a nonsmoker:

- I am the type of person who says "no" to cancer sticks.
- I am happy being smoke-free of poisonous cigarettes.
- I am happy that I no longer smell like a nasty cigarette.
- I am a successful and confident nonsmoker.
- I am happy that my lungs are clearer, and my teeth are whiter.
- I am confident I can keep gross cigarettes out of my mouth.

FUTURE PACING

We covered this concept of *future pacing* when discussing tenses. It's so important that I'd like to include it again from a slightly different angle. *Future pacing* means focusing on suggestions or images of yourself succeeding with your goal next week, next month, next year. It can be an exact time and location, or it can be a generic future time. Below are some examples you can use for public speaking:

- I see myself confidently standing in front of the civic association next Thursday at 7:00 p.m. As I begin my talk, I crack a joke about the budget, and everyone laughs.

- I see the audience applauding me as I say "thank you" to the civic association for giving me the opportunity to speak.

- I hear people saying after my talk, "That was a great speech."

- After my talk, I see everyone congratulating me on my successful speech.

- One month from now, I see my name in our club e-newsletter, saying my speech was the highlight of the event.

- I see myself feeling right at home standing on stage in front of five hundred people for our company year-end meeting.

- By next year, I envision myself as our company's number one speaker.

- By next year, I see my CEO giving me our company's excellence award for speaking and communicating.

Below are some examples you can use for weight control:

- I see myself planning healthy choices that I will be eating tomorrow.

- I notice I'm eating less tomorrow and enjoying the food more.

- _____ days from now, I will be at my goal weight of _____ pounds.

- I enjoy saying "no" to the poison known as sugar, and I confidently avoid sugar tomorrow and every day.

- I educate myself about all the food additives that contain sugar and happily say "no" to them in the future.

- I envision myself healthy, confident, and in control of food later today, tomorrow, next week, next month, and next year. I can do it!

- I see myself succeeding in my health endeavors.

WHITEBOARD TECHNIQUE

What's the *whiteboard technique*? It's the cousin of the seminar leader you learned in chapter 3. This exercise is so strong and robust that I had to include it. This approach incorporates positive thoughts and images into the subconscious via writing on a whiteboard. You imagine yourself standing in a classroom in front of a whiteboard. You'll write with the marker that you're holding in your hand.

Writing uses motor skills that were not used in the previous techniques, so a different part of the brain is activated. Earlier, we stated the fact that when you engage your imagination, the deep levels of the mind see it as reality. The writing action in this technique is another fabulous way to communicate with the subconscious program. For the first example, let's imagine you're working on feeling happy and letting go of sadness.

Imagine you're standing in front of a group of people who are interested in feeling happy. You're leading this group to help them improve their happiness. Adding the idea that *you're leading this group* also activates new neurons, the brain messengers, which then powerfully communicate building happiness.

Write the following statements on the whiteboard. As you imagine this, feel your marker in your hand and the motion as you write each letter. After you complete writing the statement, read it out loud to the group. Verbalizing this is another way of expanding your mind's success toward your goal. When you record these instructions, also give yourself time to write each statement.

Here's the first statement:

- I'm 100 percent aware that my greatest power is my power to choose my thoughts.

Again, feel your marker in your hand and the motion as you write. After you complete the statement, read it aloud.

- I welcome each new day with open arms, and I make the best out of every moment.

- I have the power and confidence to let go of the past.

- Before I close my eyes and go to sleep, I always remind myself what I'm grateful for. (You might want to include things you're grateful for such as necessities, a place to live, clothes, food, positive people in your life, the fact that you're alive, and so on.)

Continue and again feel your marker in your hand and the motion as you write. After you complete the statement, read it aloud.

- I look for ways and opportunities that I may help others.

- I have positive expectations. However, I'm not attached to any outcome, as I understand everything is unfolding as it should for my highest good.

- I play my favorite happy song often and always enjoy hearing it.

- I enjoy exercising my smile muscles every day.

- People notice how happy I am with life.

- I really appreciate life's simple pleasures.

- Acceptance is my attitude. I understand that everyone is on their own journey.

  Obviously, any of these statements could also be used in a mini self-hypnosis session.

Of note: Acceptance, according to one of my spiritual teachers, David R. Hawkins, is not passivity, or 100 percent compliance, but rather non-positionality. To me, politics is a good example. I have friends and family in both political parties. I have learned to just accept it. It's OK if we see politics differently. I have been hearing both sides of the aisle for decades say that this is the most important election of our lifetime. They say that to ignite their base. Again, the takeaway is once you accept, we are all on our journey it makes life better.

LAUGH AT THE PHOBIA THEATER

What's *phobia theater*? This is an amazing technique I came across in my studies. It puts you in a special movie theater to help you erase a fear by using laughter. Yes, laughter! For our next exercise, let's say you're afraid of mice. Envision sitting in a movie theater by yourself, feeling very calm and comfortable. You're armed with a special magic wand that can draw and create whatever you would like on the screen. As you look up at the big screen, you visualize the object of your fear on the screen. With your magic wand, use your imagination to create something funny about it.

For instance, you might imagine a cartoon image of a mouse and draw a funny picture on the mouse's face. Maybe you draw a mask or a funny beard and mustache on the face of the mouse. Maybe you put crazy eyeglasses on it, where each eye is on a big spring and pops out! Maybe you imagine something like a bold ant scaring the crap out of the mouse, and you laugh at the sight of the frightened mouse. Maybe you imagine yourself saying *boo* to the mouse, and it runs away, leaving you laughing out loud.

Imagine using sound effects or special effects that you may see or hear in a cartoon or a movie. Maybe you envision a cat as a cop coming along to arrest the mouse for not being (fill in the blank). See the mouse in jail. And laugh at the image! The idea of a mouse in jail makes you laugh and defuses any fear you may have. Use your imagination and play with this. Come up with ideas to make yourself laugh at the mouse (or whatever your fear).

This technique is a lot of fun, and you'll notice how much better you feel afterward. As a former comedian, I love how the power of laughter works in this example to diffuse a fear.

INNER ADVISER

What's an *inner adviser*? This extraordinary technique helps you receive answers to your questions. Have you ever had a situation where you were not 100 percent clear on a decision? You're not sure what to do? The inner adviser is very insightful to clarify information. You'll find "The Inner Adviser" self-hypnosis script in chapter twelve. It has helped me and many clients over the years.

AVERSION THERAPY

What's *aversion therapy*? This is using a strong feeling of dislike or disgust and attaching it to a behavior you want to change. You connect something you don't like to an action or habit that you would like to stop. This works very well for some people. For the next example, let's imagine you want to be a nonsmoker.

Most people tend to be grossed out by vomit. If you're one of them, you would tie this feeling of being grossed out to the smoking habit. You could imagine that anytime you touch a cigarette, you would be touching and smelling vomit—*eww!* Or if the smell of rotten garbage makes you nauseous, you might suggest that cigarette smoke reminds you of rotten garbage. Again, you can be as creative as you like.

You could envision tobacco leaves being dunked in vomit or feces before they make the cigarette, so when you see or smell a cancer stick, you feel like throwing up. I think you may be getting the idea by now! These suggestions work for some people. In my practice, I use them sparingly because of the negative nature of dislike. However, if I intuitively think it will help the client, I use this technique.

Even an unexpected connection can work for aversion therapy. Tom, a client in his late fifties, wanted to stop drinking alcohol. In our session, I asked, "Would you ever drink rubbing alcohol?"

He admitted that rubbing alcohol was obviously very harmful to ingest.

I asked him to imagine an image of a bottle of rubbing alcohol placed next to the alcohol that he was drinking every night, and that some rubbing alcohol was actually in both bottles. I suggested he keep looking at both bottles, and I said, "They're both bad for you to drink. True?"

A strong connection between the two bottles was formed, and it helped him say "no" to the habit. (Over the years this technique has helped many take control) The suggestion provided helped give the mental edge to be in control. After time, he did not need the rubbing alcohol reminder because he was simply in charge.

Sometimes, the simplest idea will help you get to the finish line.

If you choose to use this technique and think it will help, the key is a strong connection or association with the behavior or action you'd like to control. In the example above, I had him imagine the bottle of alcohol he drank, put the bottle next to the rubbing alcohol, and repeat the statement, "Drinking either bottle is bad for you. I say no to drinking alcohol."

See if you can come up with an idea or two for how *aversion* might assist you with your goals. My suggestion, of course, is to have fun with it.

POSTHYPNOTIC SUGGESTION

What's a *posthypnotic suggestion*? It's a mega powerful suggestion during your self-hypnosis session that's tied to an event or action that will happen *after* the session. A posthypnotic suggestion reinforces your goal by connecting it with something you're planning to do or see in the future. This is a positive way to continue to solidify your goal and to help you be successful.

What are some common everyday actions? Activities like driving a car, brushing your teeth, drinking water, putting on your slacks or jeans—whatever you can come up with will work. Then, connect the activity to a trigger, such as a color, or an object, like the sky. Here's an example of how to use this technique to overcome procrastination. If you'll be driving your car after your self-hypnosis session, say this:

Whenever I notice the color red—yes, the color red—it will remind me that *I now feel confident about getting things done.* When I see the color red, it may be a red traffic signal, or a red car, or a red taillight of the car in front of me. Red reminds me to *act on my goals.* I no longer have a to-do list, but I have a *get-it-done list!* Whenever I see the color red, it reminds me that I'm the kind of person *who gets things done.* Red says, *"I get it done."*

Or the following:

I enjoy brushing my teeth. From now on, as I'm brushing, and I feel the brush in my mouth, it reminds me how much *I enjoy getting things done.* As I clean my teeth, I like the action of the bristles against my teeth because it reminds me that I get my tasks completed. Right now, I'm completing the task of cleaning my teeth. When I'm brushing, and my taste buds notice the tooth-paste, I will say, *"I'm a person of action, and I get things done."* When standing in front of the mirror brushing my teeth, I will feel a sense of ease and confidence, knowing that *I'm mastering a task.* I no longer have a to-do list, but I have a *get-it-done list!*

Posthypnotic suggestions are one of the strongest ways to help you achieve your goals. One of the keys is to repeat the suggestions several times or more during your session. Fearlessly incorporate the suggestions into your self-hypnosis.

Five additional, powerful hypnotic techniques await you. Next chapter, please.

CHAPTER 8

READ THIS BEFORE YOU ENTER THE HYPNOSIS OFFICE

*LIFE IS A JOURNEY,
NOT A DESTINATION.*
—RALPH WALDO EMERSON

BEFORE YOU ENTER THE HYPNOSIS office (your next chapter), I'd like to introduce you to five life-changing techniques that many professional hypnotherapists use to help people pursue a positive direction. These may seem a bit technical at first, and it's OK if you don't initially understand the concepts, because you will eventually.

Being familiar with these change techniques will help you comprehend the reprogramming process for unwanted thoughts or feelings. Next, it will increase your understanding of how early childhood experiences influence your life. In addition, familiarity with these techniques may generate ideas about how you may apply them to *your* self-hypnosis. Finally, it will make reading the following chapter more enjoyable because you'll be familiar with the techniques as they're applied in an actual hypnosis session. As I said earlier, you're going to be your own hypnotherapist!

Here we go. The five techniques include regression, anchor, anchor collapse, inner child work, and chair therapy.

WHAT'S A REGRESSION?

Have you ever heard of a regression? A *regression* is a hypnotic technique during which the hypnotherapist instructs you to go back to an earlier age to recall a past event. The event may be a positive or negative experience. When you're solidly in the state of hypnosis and in the hands of a qualified hypnotherapist, this technique always delivers the event needed to work on.

I like to begin my sessions with a positive regression. The direction given to illicit a positive regression is simply, "Let's go back into your memory bank for something you did *on your own* that gave you a positive feeling, a happy feeling. This could be something that you did last week, or it may go back to your early school days. Maybe you got an A on a test, got the winning hit in a game, created art that you liked, or maybe you did something at home that made you feel very good. You'll hear a count back from ten to one, and by the time we get to number one, a positive memory will come into your mind. Something you did on your own that gave you a positive feeling." Then I just count back from ten to one, reiterating that a positive memory will come into your mind.

The therapist will then work with the positive memories using tools such as anchors (which you're going to learn about in a moment) to begin to build confidence with the client.

WHAT'S AN ANCHOR?

First, I'd like to thank motivator/author Tony Robbins, who initially introduced me to the concept of anchors. When I'm at a sporting event, standing with the crowd as I hear the national anthem being played and see the flag waving, thoughts of unity and sacrifice fill me, and I get goose bumps and feel a positive vibe. This experience is an example of an *anchor*. An anchor is a neurological response that corresponds to a specific reaction or feeling. Here are some common examples: a Christmas tree, a picture of your family, your favorite song, a memory of getting the winning hit in a baseball game, your first car, or graduation. Do you get the idea?

How about these? Seeing a colony of bees swarming around your head, flying in an airplane that is experiencing massive turbulence, or speaking in front of an audience? The feelings you have (your neurological response) that are associated with the image or sound is referred to as an *anchor*. Based on this definition, most of us have both positive and negative anchors.

Imagine if you could bottle up the feelings associated with an anchor and use them in some other time and place. You can.

What? Why would you want to do that? Because positive anchors can help you reach your goals, as you'll see. Obviously, positive anchors are good, and perceived negative anchors can get in your way.

You're going to love this, and it's *fun* to do! Let's say you have a strong positive memory anchor of achieving an A on a final exam, making the winning hit in a big game, receiving an award, or any positive memory will work. While in self-hypnosis, you focus on the positive good feelings of the memory (anchor), and as you're doing this, take your thumb and forefinger of your nondominant hand and gently press them together. Keep gently pressing your thumb and forefinger together as you're feeling your positive anchor. With practice and repetition the action of your fingers touching is creating a neurological connection.

I know this sounds easy, but the more you continue connecting the two, the stronger the connection will be. It's as if you're creating a positive switch or an anchor button. Therefore, with practice, you'll be able to take a deep breath in any situation, place your thumb and forefinger together, and choose to instantly feel great. Isn't that awesome? Yes, it is!

Why use your nondominant hand? Because that hand does not have as many hardwired neurological connections as the hand you use all the time. Therefore, it's considered easier to create a new one.

Another way of creating a positive *anchor switch* is to come up with a word or phrase that comes into your mind that represents the feelings of your positive anchor. As you're focusing on the positive feelings, let a word, a phrase, or even a color come into your mind. Some examples are the phrases "I can do it" or "I feel great" or maybe just the word "Yes!" As you repeat the words, continue focusing on the positive feelings. This repetition of the words, combined with the positive feeling, will begin to generate a very strong anchor switch for you. With practice, all you need to do is say the word or words or imagine the color, and it will bring back the feelings. Is that great or what?

Instead of a word or phrase, as I mentioned, you can also choose a color, and it works just as well. Use the color the same way you used the word or phrase to create a positive anchor. What's your favorite color? Imagine every time you think of this color or see the color that it brings back the same feelings from your positive anchor. I said this earlier, and it's true. It's fun experimenting and playing with all these techniques to see what works best for you.

Once this anchor is strongly in place, we add another one. Yes, you read that correctly. We find another positive event or experience and add it with the first one. And then, we do it again! Imagine three positive experiences in a row. This is called *stacking an anchor*. Imagine piling one good experience upon another. This creates a powerful and positive anchor button.

Let's imagine you practiced creating your own anchor button to feel calm and confident. Then a situation arises where you may feel anxious, so you take a breath; touch your thumb and forefinger together; or imagine your word, phrase, or color, and instantly you feel calm and confident. Do you think you could use a button like that?

Just to clarify, the anchor will be effective on pretty much any part of the body you choose (for instance, your hand, knuckles, a place on your arm, and so on). The location does not determine its success. I like the thumb and forefinger location because it's subtle and no one else will even know you're doing it. I've taught this technique to some fellow hypnotherapists and many clients over the years, and it's very effective.

Sometimes when working with clients we create a negative anchor button of the anxious or sad feelings. Why? Keep reading and you'll see.

WHAT'S AN ANCHOR COLLAPSE TECHNIQUE?

The goal of the *anchor collapse* is to permanently change the effect of a negative anchor. This tool helps you get rid of negative feelings. How does it work? Let me explain collapsing the anchor. Remember an anchor is a neurological response, be it positive or negative. Did you ever see one of those videos of a construction crew demolishing an old building? The building just collapses and falls to the ground. Think of that old building as the negative feeling inside you; when the building is leveled it removes the bad feelings that go with it. Yes, bad or sad feelings will be gone! This is such a GREAT technique. No pills needed, no medication—it's just using the strength of your own mind.

Here is how I set this up. After you create a positive anchor, the next step is to bring up the opposite feeling—anxiety, nervousness, or sadness. Then we lock them in (anchor it) on the hand, arm, or knuckle. One part of the body will be the negative button, and one part will be the positive button. (Creating these buttons can take some time and patience.)

Once both anchors are established (in my sessions, I usually use the clients' left and right shoulder—one positive and one negative), now we're ready to collapse the negative anchor. This is accomplished by setting them off at the exact same time. This mixes them together, which causes the negative anchor to defuse. Thus, you feel better.

After each anchor is totally established, I will say to the client, "Imagine yourself walking along a country road, and you come to a fork in the road. One path is bright and sunny, and the other is dark and cloudy. You have a life choice to make."

As I say the words "make a choice," we activate both the negative and positive anchors at the exact same time by touching the left and right shoulder simultaneously. This mixes the two buttons together (the old negative thought just crumbles and dissolves), *collapsing* the negative button to make it weak and ineffective. Then I ask, "What path did you take?"

The client always says the sunny road or the bright path. Then, to prove that the negative anchor is gone, I attempt to activate it, and ask, "Are the negative feelings gone?" The answer is usually yes, or on the very rare occasion it's not totally dissolved yet, which is OK. It just means we need to continue to work on it a bit more. Eighty percent of the time, one or two sessions eliminate a negative anchor *forever*!

Please note: the previous chapter stated that our thoughts are made up of neurons, coming together to form a hologram. My hypnosis instructors taught us that every part of the hologram contains the same information. Picture a one-dollar bill. Let's imagine this represents a thought. If we were to tear off a tiny piece of it, all the same information is in the tiny piece as is in the entire dollar. The same DNA print is on both pieces. So, both pieces are 100 percent identical on one level, no matter the size of the two pieces. Here is what this means.

Once you fire off each anchor (button) at the same time, the hologram (feeling) itself changes because you just introduced *new information to a thought*. The negative thought can *never* be the same because the neurological code has been changed. When anxious thoughts are permanently altered, the unwanted feelings will be diminished or gone. I have experienced this myself and with thousands of clients over the years. Therefore, you feel better. How cool is that? You're changing the actual construction, the blueprint of a thought! Isn't that great? This part of a session may take twenty minutes or longer. (For more detailed information about an anchor or anchor collapse, search the term *neurolinguistic programming*.)

WHAT'S INNER CHILD WORK?

Psychologytoday.com defines inner child work as "work you do either by yourself or with a therapist to resolve childhood emotions and experiences the 'inner child' still holds."

There are entire books written on this topic. I would like to give you a general idea of how I facilitate the inner child in my sessions because you'll truly benefit from this information.

Perceived hurtful experiences of our early years can create a negative feeling or "negative energy" or fear inside of us. Removing or replacing this feeling with a positive energy is the goal. This action will help the inner child feel better, safer, and loved, which results in the adult feeling *better, safer, and loved!* As you'll see, some of these ideas and techniques can be used with your self-hypnosis.

Inner child work is a vital part of healing and moving forward because most emotional issues can be traced back to childhood. How do we access the inner child? We can use regression therapy. You can connect with your inner child right now. Let me show you.

Please take a couple of slow, deep breaths. Let yourself relax. Now close your eyes and go back into your memory bank for a happy memory when you were a child. Go back, back, back to a time when you felt very happy about something as a child. Maybe it was a birthday, a new toy, or something you did with a parent or grandparent. A happy time! Maybe it was a happy memory at school. Allow some fond memory, a happy time, to come into your mind. You were smiling and happy. Do it now.

Did a happy memory come into your mind? If, for whatever reason, nothing came into your mind right now, that's OK. In an actual hypnosis session, the memories flow more easily.

We initially establish your inner child with a positive/happy memory. Now we're ready to focus on your goal. A client, Mary, age forty, will help us demonstrate the next step. She wants to overcome her paralyzing fear of public speaking.

In our session, I guide Mary to focus on the actual feelings of the anxiety she experiences while in front of an audience. When the uncomfortable feelings come up, I ask her where in her body they are. "Where do you feel them?" I ask. Typical answers are stomach, chest, or head. I have the client focus on the feelings in the body as we trace them back via a regression to when and where they began. As Mary is reliving the anxious feelings, I instruct, "Keep focusing on the feelings; we're going back to where this all started. Focus on the feeling as I count back from ten to one, and by the time we get to number one an event will come into your mind." (What comes into the client's mind is appropriately termed the *initializing event*.)

When I reach number one, I ask her, "What's coming into your mind?" And she starts describing an event from her childhood. We work on whatever comes up, and we use various hypnosis tools to help the inner child feel better and move forward.

In this example, Mary went back to elementary school to a third-grade memory, her initializing event. While she was speaking in front of the class, some of the boys made fun of her, which caused her to feel upset and nervous. This is exactly where we needed to be to begin her inner child work.

I inform Mary, "We're going to help the child feel better about this experience. I will guide you through it." I ask adult Mary to imagine herself going into the scene, and going into the third-grade class. I suggest she take little Mary off to the side and stand in front of her. The client is now looking at herself as a third grader.

I say, "Place your hands gently on little Mary's shoulders. Look her in the eye and say the following words out loud so I can hear you. Repeat these words: 'I'm you, and you're me. You're my inner child.'"

Mary then repeats the words.

I continue. "Repeat these words: 'I will always be with you, and I will always protect you, and I will always love you.'"

Mary repeats it word for word, as if she's talking directly to herself as a child.

I ask Mary, "What else can we say to this little girl to help her feel better? Is there anything else we can tell her?"

The client intuitively knows what to say, or I will make suggestions, and we continue the dialogue, such as, "You're OK now. Sometimes third-grade boys can act immature. You're OK, and you feel better now." Or, "You're going to grow up and feel confident when you speak in front of others." Or, "You'll grow up and have a wonderful life, full of love and happiness." As the conversation continues, the client experiences the inner child showing improvement about the event.

We continue the dialogue until I say, "Take the little girl in your arms and give her a nice hug until you know she feels better. You'll know when she's better because you'll see it in her face and feel it in her body. As you're hugging her, she may sigh, and her body will go limp in your arms. Take as long as she needs. Let me know when she feels better." The hypnotherapist then remains silent until this good sigh happens. It usually takes a minute or so. On a rare occasion, it may take longer for someone to work through this.

I ask, "Does the third grader look better? Does she feel better now?" The answer is always yes.

Then I suggest the following: "When I count to three, let's pretend that this never happened. Imagine that day Mary was in front of the class and everything went fine. She was a happy third grader, speaking in front of the class, feeling fine, with everything going well. Afterward, she enjoyed talking to the class."

I continue the inner child work by asking: "Wouldn't it be fun to go play with little Mary?" I suggest she imagine herself having a playdate with the little girl. Maybe she wants to take her to the beach, and she imagines herself running on the sand with the sound of the waves, or going for a bike ride, or embarking on a hike. I say, "Have fun together and imagine this now." I give this suggestion, and then I wait for a minute or so and ask what she and little Mary are doing together.

Next, I suggest that she imagine little Mary as a fourth grader, happily answering questions in class. Imagine her talking in front of the class. Then we can imagine her as a fifth grader and a sixth grader, being in front of the class and enjoying it. We continue this through high school and beyond.

This type of inner child therapy changes the neurology of the initial event and helps the client connect with herself. Any negative energy or feelings she had about public speaking diminishes or vanishes. Simply put, this work is very potently persuasive and life-changing.

I learned this technique and the next one coming up is called *chair therapy*, from the legendary hypnotherapist Jerry Kine, who's regarded as one of the best hypnosis instructors in the world. Thank you, Mr. Kine!

WHAT'S CHAIR THERAPY?

As an extension of inner child work, the goal of *chair therapy* is to create a dialogue to help the client *forgive* and *move on* from past transgressions by a specific person.

Understand that forgiveness is for ourselves and our own feelings of emotional well-being. Accepting forgiveness and letting go clears out negative emotions.

Once the client identifies who's involved with the initializing event, we imagine that person sitting in a chair six feet away. For example, if a parent or adult did something that caused your initializing event, they would be included in this therapy. The therapist then directs a conversation between the client and the other person or persons. The client shares his or her experience, expressing how the person's or persons' actions (or lack of) felt. This exchange will lead to forgiveness and letting go.

Sandy, age thirty-six, will help us with this. Sandy became nauseous every time she tried to drink water. Sandy recalls having this issue for her entire life. For health reasons and just to feel more normal, she wanted to drink water and enjoy it like everyone else. A permanent memory event from her early childhood revealed the psychological cause. Eight-year-old Sandy was having an argument with her father about drinking water. She told her father she did not want to drink any water.

Her father said, "You'll drink water." He angrily grabbed her and pulled her to the kitchen sink and physically forced a glass of water down her throat. This upsetting action made her throw up and feel scared.

At this stage in the session, we already did the previous inner child work, where the adult Sandy talked with her and calmed her down. Now it's time for chair therapy. I say, "Imagine eight-year-old Sandy is sitting in a chair. Six feet away from you is your father sitting in a chair. Look your father in the eye and tell him out loud how his actions made you feel. Say it out loud so I can hear you."

Sandy spoke directly to her father. "It was horrible and frightening. I felt scared. To be treated like this was the most horrible experience of my life. It made me feel sad."

I then take my finger and gently touch Sandy's forehead, between her eyes, in an area known as the *third eye*. I gently tap this area, and say, "You're now the dad. You're now the father. Why did you do this to your daughter? Why are you acting so cruel? What's the matter with you?" Then the client talks as if they're the father. Most of the time, the responses are, "I was wrong," "I'm sorry," "It was a bad thing to do," and so on.

Then I tap Sandy's forehead again, and say, "You're now the eight-year-old girl, your dad says it was wrong for him to do this, and he is sorry." We continue the conversation back and forth until we arrive at forgiveness and letting go.

On the rare occasion when the dad (or whoever caused the problem) responds like a jerk and says mean or disparaging remarks like, "She has to do what she's told," the therapist will intervene. The therapist will point out that, despite what their reason is to act like this—usually related to their own childhood experiences—it's unproductive and not nice to treat people in this manner. There are more constructive ways to communicate, and a better choice of words or actions is needed. Eventually, we arrive at the same destination, which is forgiveness and letting go.

These change techniques have helped my clients erase decades of emotional pain, many times in just one session.

Now it's time to "come into my hypnosis office." Next page, please.

CHAPTER 9

COME INTO MY HYPNOSIS OFFICE

WHEN THE STUDENT IS READY, THE TEACHER WILL APPEAR.
—BUDDHA SIDDHARTHA

IT'S TIME FOR YOU TO journey into a professional hypnosis office. This chapter will give you a firsthand understanding of what occurs during one of my typical sessions to help people make a positive change in their life, including the pre-talk (initial conversation), the hypnotic induction, discovering the *why*, various therapies, posthypnotic suggestions, and more. This open look at what transpires will show you the awesome power we all possess to move forward.

What's the single most important element for success in hypnotherapy? The number one ingredient is the client's desire to change. If your spouse wants you to come in for something and you really don't want to, well, stay home. Over the years I have had a few requests where the client wanted to make an appointment for their spouse, and I say, "Sorry, they must make their own appointments."

To be a great hypnotherapist you need to be both a skilled mechanic and an artist. When you bring your car in for inspection, there are specific guidelines the mechanic follows. The hypnotherapist has a "recipe" or a "script" to help someone stop smoking, control his or her weight, or enhance a specific skill. Hypnotherapists who follow a script and can also work in a creative manner to *individualize* the experience will produce fabulous results for their clients.

Let's imagine you're coming to my office for help with public speaking anxiety. Many people are trepidatious and anxious about speaking in front of others. A survey of college students indicated that the number one fear was public speaking, and death was second! (The first case study in the next chapter is about this issue, which will help give you another vantage point for the same goal.) Before I see each client, whether in my office or virtually, my ritual is to say a prayer and ask for guidance to help them achieve their goal. For the purpose of following examples, we will assume it's an in-person session.

As you walk into my hypnosis office to overcome the fear of public speaking, I will immediately use a *waking suggestion*. This type of suggestion relates to an action you're about to do, such as sitting down. As you enter and we exchange greetings, you'll hear soft, relaxing music in the background and notice a comfortable recliner. Now I deliver my waking suggestion. I point to the recliner and say, "That chair helps you feel more confident when speaking in front of others, so grab a seat." Do you see what just happened? It's very subtle. As you sit down, you've already received a suggestion for success.

I usually begin a session with small talk about where you live or ask a question about your occupation. Then we move into a discussion about the reason you're here. I acquire background information and any other goals you may have. I let you know that at one time in my life, I was sitting exactly where you are: in front of a hypnotherapist. Therefore, I can appreciate how you may be feeling. During our conversation, whenever applicable, I may also look for something that we may be able to laugh about, as laughter is therapeutic and helps build rapport. I ask lots of questions like, "Have you always felt this way? Why do you want to change? How will this change benefit you? Can you think of any specific incident that may have led you to have this fear? Is this a work-related issue or something else? How would you like to feel when you're speaking in front of others? What will you be speaking to people about?"

To assess their current confidence level, I ask, "On a scale from one to ten, with ten representing a very positive and confident speaker, what number are you today?" The response is a low number, either one, two, or three. I make a note of this, because, at the end of the session, I will ask the same question to gauge how much better and more confident they feel, which is also a reflection of the therapeutic value of our session.

I continue to ask questions and introduce the basic truths of your mind: "What's your greatest power? What are the two most important words you think or say? What's the number one trait of your mind?" (Sound familiar?) We talk for approximately forty-five minutes, and I take notes on the responses.

A good therapist pays specific attention to an individual's speech patterns, which provide them information about the client's dominant learning mode. Is it visual, kinesthetic, or auditory? For example, if the client uses phrases like, "I hear you," "That sounds great," or "Listen to this," they like the auditory channel, so I will approach the process more from that standpoint.

Most people assume that during a hypnosis session, the therapist is talking and the client is sitting back with their eyes closed listening. Nothing could be further from the truth. In my office, there is a lot of back-and-forth while the client is in hypnosis, because when it's done correctly, the interaction between us multiplies the value of the process. You're answering various questions, and then there may be times when I have you open your eyes, and we talk for a short while. Throughout the session I continue to give you suggestions that you'll feel calm and relaxed. I also ask you to repeat certain statements and use your imagination in various ways to reach your goal.

I make an audio recording of your session, using the audio file on your cell phone, which is available to you afterward to use for reinforcement, if needed. When I follow up with clients, most say they never needed the audio recording; however, some have reported that they did listen and found it helpful.

After I've answered any questions and gleaned all the background information I need, you're ready to adventure into one of the most relaxing experiences ever: a professional hypnotherapy session.

I always start our session by saying, "Let me show you exactly how we're going to do this" and then we'll actually do it.

Let's pretend you're sitting in the comfortable recliner across from me. We just had a nice chat about you and your goal. I hand you a pair of headphones since I'll be speaking through a microphone. Using a sound system has been proven to enhance the positive power of the experience, as opposed to just talking.

Once the headphones are in place, you hear my voice clearly (I'm right in your head, so to speak). Before we start the session, I say, "Let me show you what this is going to be like before we actually begin. All you need to do is simply follow my instructions to the best of your ability."

Then I say:

"Let's begin by taking a couple of slow deep breaths. Please inhale and exhale through your nose and take a nice deep breath and let it out slowly through your nose. Take another big deep breath and fill up your lungs as deeply as you can and hold it. And when you exhale, allow your eyes to gently close. With your eyes closed, gently nod your head *yes, please*. That's good. With your eyes closed, raise your right index finger on your right hand and put it back down. Gently nod your head *yes, please*. Good. I will count to three in a moment. When you hear the number three, you'll take the headphones off, jump up out of the chair, run over to the corner of the room, stand on top of your head, and scream as loudly as you can, 'I'm the greatest! I'm the greatest! I'm the greatest!'"

At this point, you might open your eyes slightly, maybe crack a slight smile or chuckle, or even give me a strange look. I respond with:

"Notice how well you did the breathing; notice how well you closed your eyes; notice how well you lifted your index finger, and you nodded your head; but when I gave a ridiculous suggestion like standing on your head and screaming, you were not going to follow that suggestion. *You decide what you'll accept. Now you see that you're in charge here, and I'm just the guide.*"

I confirm that you're comfortable and ready to start. Step one is the *induction*, getting you into a focused trance or hypnotic state. There are several types of inductions. The most common one used in hypnotherapy offices is called a *progressive relaxation*. This is the one I prefer and the only one I refer to in this book. It's a process of guiding you to deeper levels of relaxation by simply highlighting different points of the body and having you imagine these areas relaxing. I speak in a slow, soothing voice as I'm guiding you.

You feel so relaxed, it's as if you're sinking into the recliner and your muscles are just kind of sagging, like a loose, limp rag doll.

Most people report that they feel a comfortable heaviness or a light, floating feeling. Initially, I spend time having you imagine different parts of your body feeling very relaxed. Then you imagine you're walking down a very special stairway, the stairway of relaxation, which has ten steps. Each step down takes you into deeper levels of relaxation. By the time you reach the bottom of the stairway, you feel very, very relaxed and comfortable.

Or instead of the stairway, I may suggest that you're standing in front of a whiteboard on which you see the number ten. I count down from ten to one. As each number appears on the board, you erase it. Each number you erase brings you to a deeper level of relaxation. The lower you go, the more relaxed you feel.

Once we arrive at the bottom of the steps, I continue with more relaxing or deepening techniques. At this point you're feeling very relaxed. I suggest that you find a safe place, a place where you feel very comfortable and secure, a location where you feel 100 percent calm and peaceful. I've found it very interesting to hear some of my clients' safe places. Most report that it's a room in their house, typically their bedroom. It may be a room, a place from their childhood, or a special place in nature. Once in a great while, a client comments that their safe place is totally imaginary, like a special room with white light or that they're floating on a cloud.

At this point, you're officially in a focused mental state, which gives us access to your subconscious. Hypnotherapists agree that people can reach three levels of hypnotic depth: light, medium, and heavy. Effective work can be done at all three levels. Most people easily get to the medium level.

To prove that you're truly in a hypnotic state, I can do simple tests called "convincers." One of these is to suggest that your arm feels so heavy and so comfortable that it just wants to stay right there and not move. You try to move it, but it won't cooperate because it's so perfectly comfortable. Another test may be to have you imagine that your eyelids feel so heavy and so sleepy that your eyes won't open because they feel so good being closed.

I suggest, "When you have a sense of what it feels like when your eyelids are so tired and heavy that it would be too much effort to open them, just nod your head." This demonstrates that you're in the hypnotic state. Remember that when you're in the hypnotic state, the doorway to your subconscious is open. Then it's time to reprogram your mind so you can achieve your desired goal.

Let's get back to you in the recliner, relaxing in that nice, deep trance state. I usually begin the therapeutic part of the session with some general, direct suggestions of success for your specific goal. I follow this by helping you regress into your memory bank to identify some positive memories from earlier in life.

This is where we build the positive anchor you read about in the previous chapter.

Once the positive anchor is locked in, it's time to find out *why* or the reason you don't feel confident speaking in public.

The *why* is always at the root of the client's distress, anxiety, and negative beliefs. Most of the time, people don't know the exact reason for their situation.

The next chapter (case studies) are examples of the *why*. Regression is used to discover the why, to take you to the initializing event. At this point, I suggest that you bring back the anxious feelings about speaking in front of people. I ask where in your body you're feeling the anxiety. The response is usually in the chest or stomach area, sometimes the head or arms. Now I ask you to focus on those feelings while I count back from ten to one to trace how this originated. As you're solidly in the hypnotic state, I suggest staying focused on the anxious feelings as I count back. When I reach number one, the information and the why will come forward and we work on whatever surfaces. We then proceed to reframe the why with various tools such as inner child work, anchor collapse, chair therapy, and the like.

Once the why is reframed in the subconscious (depending on the client, this part of the session may take twenty to forty minutes), it is time to suggest you imagine yourself speaking confidently in front of others next week, next month, and next year (this you may recall from chapter 7 is called *future pacing*). You see yourself standing self-assuredly in front of the audience. You imagine someone commenting to you afterward that your presentation was outstanding and saying you did a great job!

Now it's time for a repeat technique. I ask you to repeat positive affirmations of courage, confidence, and success.

Suppose that earlier in our conversation, you mentioned how much you like sunny days. I will then deliver a posthypnotic suggestion that when you experience a sunny day, it reminds you of your new and increased confidence talking in front of others.

I suggest that in the future, any feelings you may have before speaking ("butterflies") will feel like happy excitement as opposed to nervousness.

When you're excited about something, your mental approach and motivation will shift. The *Journal of Experimental Social Psychology* cited a study of college graduates in 2010. When the participants simply shifted their focus to excitement about speaking, they felt and performed better. In other words, you know those butterflies you have in your stomach before you're about to speak or go on stage. You tell yourself those are just excited feelings and you can't wait to get out there to share your message with the audience. Question: Was the ability of these college grads to change their focus to excitement also an example of them using their greatest power to choose? *Yes, it was.*

We're just about finished with your session. I have you imagine a scale from one to ten, with ten being the most confident speaker you could possibly be. I say, "When you came into the office, the number was very low, but now, imagine a scale from one to ten and see a new number. Can you see a number of how confident you are now?" Most of the time, the client says nine or ten; the number always goes up from where they started.

We conclude the session by bringing you back up to waking consciousness. I give the instruction, "I will count from one to five, and by the time we reach the number five, you'll be wide awake and alert, feeling great."

Then we chat for a little bit to see how good you feel. The office visit usually takes about two hours or more. You also now have an audio file of the session. I follow up with a phone call to you the next day and again a week or so later to see how you're doing. Most clients never need to come back for another session because they've achieved their goal.

Coming up next: details on how hypnosis changed my clients' lives.

CHAPTER 10

SUCCESSFUL SUBCONSCIOUS CASE STUDIES

I DON'T CARE HOW MUCH POWER, BRILLIANCE, AND ENERGY YOU HAVE. IF YOU DON'T FOCUS IT ON A SPECIFIC TARGET AND HOLD IT THERE, YOU'RE NEVER GOING TO ACCOMPLISH AS MUCH AS YOUR ABILITY WARRANTS.
—ZIG ZIGLAR

HERE ARE SOME INSPIRING TRUE stories from my hypnosis practice, which I hope will enhance your appreciation and understanding of the benefits of tapping into yourself with hypnosis. I think you'll find them interesting, enlightening and, in some cases, familiar because we've already mentioned them earlier in the book.

CASE STUDY 1—THE GOAL: BE A CONFIDENT SPEAKER

Mary, age forty, had recently been promoted at her job and would be leading small meetings (six to ten people). She said, "I'm terrified, and I have so much anxiety over this. I don't know what I'm going to do! Can hypnosis help?"

I assured her that it could. I asked her if she knew why she had such strong negative feelings about speaking in front of others.

She said, "I don't know. As far as I can remember, I've always been afraid to speak in front of others. In school, I never wanted to even raise my hand in class to answer any questions!" On a scale of one to ten, with ten being the most confident, her self-confidence level in public speaking was a one.

I guided her into a relaxed trance state. We focused on some positive life experiences, and we created a positive anchor. Then it was time to find out why she was so anxious in front of others. We did a regression to find out what event had sparked such anxiety. She recalled an incident while she was speaking in front of her third-grade class. Some of the kids were teasing and making fun of her. She felt embarrassed. At that age, the taunts made an indelible impression, and this was where it all began.

The next step was to do therapy on the *why*, the "initializing event" of being embarrassed and teased. The therapy included inner child work, chair therapy, forgiveness, and an anchor collapse of the negative anxious feelings. We also imagined the initial event had a different outcome. We had Mary see herself feeling calm and confident as a school child all through elementary school and beyond. That was followed by more regression work to make sure there was no other event or incident impeding her from reaching her goal. Nothing else came up.

I suggested that she see herself feeling calm and confident as an adult. Then I made some direct suggestions for her success and confidence. She imagined herself feeling calm and confident while leading these meetings. We did some repetition of positive "I am" statements out loud. Her affection for sunny days was the perfect opportunity to use as a posthypnotic suggestion for successful, confident public speaking.

We wrapped it up with asking her, "On a scale from one to ten, how do you feel now about public speaking and leading the groups at work?"

"Nine," she replied.

Do you remember that when I initially asked her why she was so anxious about public speaking, the client did not consciously recall the third-grade event? Most of the time, clients are not exactly sure what caused their specific anxiety, but during a hypnosis session, we always find it. We completed this session in about an hour and forty-five minutes. That's all the work she needed to become very successful with her new position and her future. No more sessions were needed.

CASE STUDY 2—THE GOAL: RELIEVE PANDEMIC ANXIETY

This was a Skype session with Jim, a thirty-seven-year-old businessman. He could not stop worrying about COVID-19. He was happily married with a three-year-old child, and he was laid off from his job due to the pandemic; his wife was still employed. Because he was out of work, he found himself continually monitoring social media and the news, reading all the latest updates on the virus. The more he read, the more anxious he felt. He kept asking himself, "What if I don't get my job back? What if I or my loved ones get the virus? How are we going to pay our bills? Why did this have to happen?" He was also not sleeping well.

Once he entered the hypnotic state, we worked on positive anchors. I had him focus on his greatest power, which, as you know, is the power to choose your own thoughts. I asked him a series of questions designed to make him realize that he was OK. Based on the initial discussion we had prior to the hypnosis session, I knew what most of his answers were going to be. Sometimes it's simply a matter of asking the right questions to refocus the client's mind. What follows is a good example of how this works.

My first question was: "Have you done everything you can to protect your wife and family during the pandemic?" He said yes. Next question: "Do you think this pandemic will ever end?" He said yes. Next, I asked: "In the worst-case scenario, if you or your wife came down with the virus, do you think your family would survive?" Again, he said yes. Then I asked, "Do you understand that you've done everything in your power to protect your wife and family?" He again answered yes. Finally, I asked, "You know this pandemic will end, right?" He replied that yes, he did. See how these questions helped to shift his focus?

I also suggested that he ask himself a new set of questions, for example:

- What can I do to help my wife?
- What am I thankful for right now?
- Are there any projects I can do around the house?
- With my extra time at home, what would I like to teach my three-year-old (numbers, colors, animals, shapes)?

The answers to these questions helped ease Jim's mind and essentially released the fear. I also referred to his strong business skills, reinforcing the reality that he was talented and, in time, would find a new job.

I also recommended that Jim take a break from the news and social media for a few days (which is good advice for all of us). I suggested that he imagine himself laughing and having fun later that day and the next day as the first step toward enjoying his time at home during the pandemic. These visualizations helped him to relax and feel good. I continued with a suggestion that he read an enjoyable book or watch a favorite movie.

He repeated positive "I am" statements such as:

- I am confident in my abilities to use my greatest power to choose.
- I now choose to feel calm about the pandemic.
- I now choose positive, loving thoughts.
- I now choose to believe my family will survive, and we will come out stronger than ever.
- I have the power to turn off the news.

- I'm feeling great about my life.
- I'm thankful for my wife and child.
- I'm thankful for my positive outlook.
- I'm thankful for our house.
- I'm thankful for our good health.
- I'm thankful for our food.
- I'm the type of person who can confidently accept any challenge that comes my way.
- I'm courageous and confident.

After one session, Jim reported no anxiety about the virus and said he was doing great. In addition, the session created a positive ripple effect in all aspects of the client's life and positively impacted those around him.

CASE STUDY 3—THE GOAL: FEEL NORMAL WHEN DRIVING

Lisa was a client in my second year of hypnotherapy work in 1996. The thirty-five-year-old woman had anxiety about driving. I asked her to tell me about the problem.

She explained, "If I know where I'm going, I'm OK, I'm fine, but if I don't know where the place is, or if I've never been there, I get very, very anxious. Next week I need to take my daughter to a cheerleading competition, and just thinking about it has me feeling anxious and nervous. It's become so bad that I have to get someone else to drive us!"

I asked her how long this fear had been plaguing her, and she said, "I've always felt a little uncomfortable driving, but as I've gotten older, it has just gotten worse."

I asked her if she knew why this was happening. She said no.

We started our session by establishing a positive anchor and so on. We then went back to the initializing event. When she was ten, she was in the backseat of a car with her parents, headed to Myrtle Beach, South Carolina, for a vacation. Her ten-year-old girlfriend she'd invited was sitting next to her. It was late at night, and her parents got lost (before the days of GPS). As a result, her parents got into an argument that escalated into out-of-control screaming, yelling, and cursing. She was witnessing the most powerful people she knew, her parents, engaged in a terrifying fight. She was scared and embarrassed that her friend was also experiencing this meltdown, and this frightening incident was taking place *in a car bound for an unfamiliar destination.*

This repressed memory event was the cause of her anxiety. To help reconfigure and reframe this experience, we did inner child work, chair therapy, forgiving the parents, and imagining the situation resulting in a more positive outcome. We also did some direct suggestions of success and confidence, followed by having her imagine herself driving safely and confidently anywhere she wants to go.

The session took about two hours. Reframing that initializing event successfully freed her to drive anywhere. One session and done!

CASE STUDY 4—THE GOAL: OVERCOME CLAUSTROPHOBIA

Forty-four-year-old Joanne came to my office wanting to deal with claustrophobia. Her fear of being closed in was so strong that she asked me to keep the office door open. I asked her how long this had been going on. She knew exactly what had started it: she was nine, and her brothers closed her in an old refrigerator that was going to be picked up and taken away. They had her get in and then closed the door on her. (Brothers!)

Her hypnotherapy session included inner child work, chair therapy, forgiveness, and imagining that it had not happened. This work allowed her to let go of the negative feelings and release them. I suggested that she see herself controlling her thoughts in any situation that might, in the past, have triggered a claustrophobic reaction. We focused on her ability to feel safe and be able to breathe anywhere, anytime, anyplace. I delivered direct suggestions about her success and confidence to her subconscious.

As soon as the session was over, I closed the office door and asked, "How do you feel about that door being closed now?"

She said, *"Great!* I'm OK now." One session was all she needed to let it go.

CASE STUDY 5—THE GOAL: BE ASSERTIVE WHEN NEEDED

I received a call from a client who I had previously assisted with weight control. She asked if hypnosis could help her husband with assertiveness. I said yes, but to please have her husband contact me to schedule. Each individual must take responsibility to initiate the process. The forty-two-year-old husband, David, contacted me and scheduled an appointment for assertiveness.

We worked on reprogramming his subconscious so that he could understand it's OK that he can speak up for himself and display assertiveness without being rude or disrespectful. We also did some inner child work and used the modeling technique of someone he deemed as confident and assertive. Then we did direct suggestions of success and confidence. David repeated the "I am" calm-and-assertive mantra. The first session lasted about ninety minutes, and the second session a week later was a little over an hour.

Six months later—yes, six months—I got a call from his wife, who had referred him. "I cannot believe it," she said, "but we were at the mall yesterday, and this situation came up in which my husband was able to assert himself. It was amazing to see him like that. I had to tell you and thank you."

CASE STUDY 6—THE GOAL:
IMPROVE GOLF PERFORMANCE

Ray, a fifty-three-year-old chap, needed help with his golf game, specifically his putting. Whenever he needed to putt, his wrists would involuntarily start to shake, causing him to miss even the easiest stroke. (In golf this is called the *yips.*) Ray was frustrated, because he was an accomplished athlete who had excelled at a variety of sports. And although he was an accomplished golfer, once he started shaking, all he could think about was, "Is this shaky syndrome going to happen again?" Remember what I said earlier: what you think about, you bring about.

I helped him go back in his memory to a time when he was putting successfully. We projected that success into the present and the future. I also suggested that Ray remember to *have fun* playing golf. I further suggested that he approach each putt feeling relaxed and confident. We came up with a simple five-step process:

1. Assess

2. Visualize

3. Visualize again

4. Cleansing breath

5. Perform

Before Ray hits the ball, he looks over the shot (*assess*), determines what to do, visualizes himself standing over the ball (*visualize*), takes a deep breath, and imagines a smooth stroke to sink the putt. Then he addresses the ball by standing over the ball, visualizes the shot going in again (*visualize again*), then takes a deep breath (*cleansing breath*), and exhales and then putts (*performs*). Once the shot is taken, he accepts the result and moves on. Repeatedly, Ray visualizes himself with a relaxed and confident approach to putting.

We also created an anchor with a few of his confident memories and used those feelings toward success with his new relaxed putting game. Bye-bye, shaky wrists. Welcome back, good golf game. One session and done! Fun fact: Ray later changed his name and joined the pro golf tour. You might know him by his new name, Tiger Woods. (And that, my friend, is fun fiction.)

CASE STUDY 7—THE GOAL: FEEL GLAD INSTEAD OF SAD

Ron, thirty-seven, sometimes felt very sad when he was alone. He also had never been able to sustain a long-term romantic relationship. He had, however, been very successful in business. He believed his sad feelings had originated at a very young, vulnerable age. His parents were separated by the time he was a toddler. He was raised by his mother, and he had no relationship with his father, whom he recalled seeing maybe half a dozen times in his entire life.

During the one and only overnight visit with his father, while he was a fourth grader, Ron had a very negative experience. He does not recall having any contact with his father after that. Five years later, while he was in ninth grade, his aunt told Ron his father had died of a heart attack. At the funeral, total strangers approached him to say they were sorry about his dad's passing. It was an emotional event for him, but at the same time, he found it very disorienting; he had not really known his father. He had a lot of underlying emotions, including neglect, resentment, and sadness.

We did four sessions, which included extensive inner child work, chair therapy, forgiveness, letting go of the past, and positive "I am" statements. We also did anchors and an anchor collapse. After our first session, I recommended reading *The Power Is Within You* by Louise Hay. With each session he felt an incremental improvement. I also pointed out that parents do the best they can with what they have. None of us really know what our parents' lives were like when they were young. Everyone is on their own journey in this game of life. Inner child work in situations like Ron's can produce powerful results. Learning how to let go of a past negative experience and forgiving those involved can be equally powerful.

After a few sessions, Ron began to feel like a new man. My long-term follow-up found him happily married with three children. He commented that our hypnosis work was the best thing he'd ever done for himself. He said it brought him clarity, erased his sadness, and left him with a "clean slate" of mind.

He added, "When I look at my life, having had a father who did not understand the emotional impact he could have, this void in my childhood made me much more aware of my actions and intentions as a parent. My goal was to be 180 degrees opposite of my dad in parenting, as a husband, and as a man." Ron succeeded big-time in reaching that goal.

CASE STUDY 8—THE GOAL: TO EAT NORMAL FOOD

A nineteen-year-old college student named William would not eat anything but chicken. He ate only chicken wings, thighs, and breasts, plus chicken loaf and chicken nuggets. That meant no fruit, no vegetables, no pizza. No *pizza?* Yep. This had started in middle school and had been going on for years. His parents tried to have him eat other foods, but he could not get other foods past his lips. Now that he was in his first year of college, he wanted to expand his dietary options. He wanted to be able to eat the same foods his friends enjoyed. During our session, we did not discover a stunning emotional issue as the cause.

To help him achieve the confidence, he needed to change his diet. I had him focus on new things he'd accomplished in the past couple of years, like driving a car, going on dates, and attending college. We also focused on previous successes that he had. I suggested he was ready for some new flavors that he would enjoy, allowing his taste buds to have fun again and experience variety. I further suggested that he imagine himself eating pizza and really liking it.

What William did not know was that I had planned to have pizza delivered to my office. After we accomplished a lot of work in the session, I said, "When I count to three, you'll open your eyes, and I will hand you a slice of pizza, and you'll take a bite and see if you like it."

I handed him an actual slice; he took a bite, and he liked it. I even recorded a short video of him eating the slice of pizza. Ten minutes later, we did the same thing with a banana. He closed his eyes and we affirmed that he could eat whatever he wanted. I ended the session and showed him the videos. William could now happily eat a variety of foods. Because it included a lunch break, this was a little over a two-hour session.

CASE STUDY 9—THE GOAL: DRINK WATER

Sandy, a thirty-six-year-old office worker, became nauseated every time she tried to drink water. She recalled having this issue her entire life. For health reasons and to feel more normal, she wanted to drink water and enjoy it like everyone else.

During her session, she recalled a permanent memory event from her childhood that revealed the cause. Eight-year-old Sandy was having an argument with her father about drinking water. She told him she did not want to drink any. Her father angrily grabbed her, pulled her to the kitchen sink, and forced a glass of water down her throat. This had made her throw up and is clearly the initializing event.

Now that she had identified this painful memory, we worked on reframing it. I used inner child work, chair therapy, letting go, anchor collapse, forgiving her father, and imagining the situation having a more positive outcome. I gave her direct suggestions for success and confidence, followed by having her imagine drinking water whenever she wanted to and enjoying it.

Toward the end of the session, I had her open her eyes and I handed her a bottle of water, which she began drinking. After a long swig, she smiled and said she was very much enjoying it. (I captured this triumph on video and showed it to her at the end of the session.) We continued with lots of positive "I am" statements, such as "I have the personal power to let go of the past. I'm a happy water drinker. I like the feeling of water in my mouth. I see myself enjoying a glass of water." This life-changing moment was completed in just one session!

CASE STUDY 10—THE GOAL: STOP SMOKING

Jon, a successful forty-seven-year-old executive, wanted to stop smoking. He had smoked for thirty-one years. He said, "I cannot quit smoking. I have been successful in so many areas of my life, but I'm having the hardest time trying to quit. I quit for a day or two and then I go right back."

I said, "I see you've been a success in your business career," and asked, "Do you consider yourself a quitter?"

"No," he said immediately.

Because of his strong resistance to quitting anything, he needed a different linguistic approach. He needed to frame it differently. I asked, "Why not just *stop smoking*, and let's take the idea of *quitting* out of the equation?"

He paused, nodded, smiled, and said yes. Once this idea was in his mind, he was easily able to stop.

The session included positive anchors and a regression back to when he first started smoking. We did inner child work and had him imagine that did not smoke that day. We focused on how smoking causes cancer and sickness. He now chooses to be healthy. We did some aversion therapy. We did positive statements that were repeated out loud, with him saying, "I stop cancer sticks now and forever. I choose health over cancer sticks."

He created images of seeing himself smoke-free today, tomorrow, and next week, images of himself being offered cigarettes and him saying, "No, I'm a nonsmoker!" I included posthypnotic suggestions using the color red and the act of brushing his teeth, reinforcing his status as a nonsmoker. After a one hour and forty-five-minute session, he was indeed a happy nonsmoker.

CASE STUDY 11—THE GOAL: TO SPEED HEALING OF A SPORTS HERNIA

Rich, forty-one, was a computer programmer who loved sports and considered himself a weekend warrior. He participated in various sports leagues, including softball, basketball, and soccer. He also lifted weights. During the summer of 1996, Rich suffered a sports hernia, which is a painful, soft tissue injury in the lower abdominal region, including muscle fiber tears. After two months of not completely healing, he was willing to try just about anything to help him get back to his activities. He thought he would try hypnosis.

Our plan was a healing hypnosis session that I recorded for him. I suggested that he refrain from any physical activity for two weeks, and that he use the audio file once or twice each day. In the session, various creative healing strategies were used to motivate his cells to mend the soft tissue.

He envisioned the blood vessels opening in the lower abdominal region so that more blood could travel through that area. He pretended he was a scuba diver whose mission was to repair the underbelly of a boat (for you boat enthusiasts, that's the *hull*). He imagined himself applying adhesive to the damage underneath the boat and seeing it look better and being repaired. He even imagined that he had magical knitting needles stitching the muscle fibers together and envisioned himself completely healed. He followed through with the instructions, and the sports hernia was finally healed. Self-hypnosis was a great tool to aid in the healing process!

WHY POSITIVE EXPECTATIONS WORK

Did you notice that, in most people's experiences prior to the session, they were often focused on negative outcomes? Those thoughts naturally create anxiety. Remember the number one trait of your mind: (fill in the blanks, please) you g_ i_ t__ d_____ o_ y__ t_____.

In all these cases, the single most important element of the client's success was choosing to *take action* through hypnosis. Making a positive choice is admirable. We all know some people who complain, make excuses for themselves, and tend to be negative. When you combine positive action, self-determination, and a commitment to your goal, you'll achieve success. Self-hypnosis is the perfect tool for change.

In the next chapter, you'll learn something that is positively life-changing.

CHAPTER 11

LEARN THIS AND LIFE IS A BREEZE

GOD, GRANT ME THE SERENITY TO ACCEPT
THE THINGS I CANNOT CHANGE;
COURAGE TO CHANGE THE THINGS I CAN;
AND WISDOM TO KNOW THE DIFFERENCE.
—REINHOLD NIEBUHR, SERENITY PRAYER

ONE OF THE BENEFITS OF working through a book like this is not only acquiring a basic understanding of how the mind works, but you begin to see yourself with new eyes and have a feeling of greater control of yourself and acceptance the world around you.

MY EPIPHANY, AKA MY AHA MOMENT

If what I'm about to share with you has just half of the impact as it did on me, it will be happily beneficial for you. Here is my life-changing moment.

Sometimes we're ready for the right words or phrase that may give us some awakening insight and clarity; here is mine. In 2019, I was listening to one of my spiritual teachers, author David R. Hawkins, who said the following, "The universe and all of life is in a constant state of creation and evolution. Creation and evolution are the same. Everything, everything is unfolding exactly as it should. Who are you to say it should not be this way? You're going to tell the creator of the universe it should not be this way?"

Let me repeat this for you: "The universe and all of life is in a constant state of creation and evolution. Creation and evolution are the same. Everything, everything is unfolding exactly as it should. Who are you to say it should not be this way? You're going to tell God it should not be this way?"

Everything is unfolding as it should. What? I never thought of it that way. When I heard him say that it hit me! I thought, *You mean, I was supposed to have that biological father who never gave me a birthday or Christmas card* (acceptance)? *I was supposed to get injured on my construction job in 1973* (acceptance)? *I was supposed to get divorced in 1991* (acceptance)? *I was supposed to be screwed out of that money in 1993* (acceptance)? *On November 3, 1995, I was supposed meet the woman of my dreams, and I was supposed to end up with three beautiful, talented children, and now have three grandchildren* (acceptance)?

Yes! And get this: you're supposed to be reading this right now!

It was my *aha* moment of acceptance! *Oh my God, I get it!* My entire body felt this sense of release that was palpable. The message of this quote rings loud and clear to me: *acceptance!* Everyone is on their own journey here, and we have to accept that. If you don't, it can create negative vibrations inside you that are truly unhealthy. I have heard many spiritual teachers and motivational masters say that we're nothing but energy. Each person is just their own energy field or their own personal vibration of energy.

This reminds me of the famous quote by the philosopher Nietzsche, who said, "What doesn't kill me makes me stronger." I believe the attitude of acceptance keeps you resilient and helps you overcome any adversity. Yes, it does!

It may seem a bit strange to say this, but over time the TV news helped me become more aware of the concept of acceptance. Let me explain. The news business tends to be driven more by ratings than reality; but when I was younger, I naively believed that whatever was said in the media was true. This led me to have some negative and fearful thinking, as most of the headlines were life altering. I'd like to share some examples of the news stories I'm referring to:

BAD NEWS OF 1970S, 1980S, 1990S, AND 2000S

1970s

- The book *The Population Bomb* by Paul Ehrlich was a big topic on talk shows in the early '70s. The message was that, due to population growth, they predicted by the year 2000 that worldwide famine was expected, because farming would not meet the demand for food. We were told that we would have riots in the streets, because there would be too many people and not enough to eat. The future was bleak.

- In 1975, *Time* magazine and all news broadcasts reported that climate scientists claimed a "new Ice Age" was on its way. Lower temperatures were predicted, and by the year 2000 or sooner, New York City was expected to be a sheet of ice. Let me say that again: they said that by the year 2000 or sooner, New York City would be a sheet of ice, and that food and energy shortages would cause anarchy. The future was bleak.

- News broadcasts reported that oil shortages would cause major disruptions in life. The future was bleak.

1980s

- News broadcasts reported that acid rain would destroy all plants and that the future was bleak.

- The BBC in 1985 predicted that ozone depletion would cause cancer and immune deficiency worldwide.

1990s

- Global warming was predicted to cause the end of life as we know it on planet Earth. The future was said to be bleak. Remember that twenty years earlier they said we were all going to die because the Earth was going to freeze to death.

2000s

- Global warming morphed into "climate change," and so now, whether it's cold or hot, *you're still going to die!* Ha ha!

Gloom and doom sell. However, to be fair, in some cases it may be difficult to access accurate information that has been denied, sometimes by those who might benefit. For example, many years ago there were cover-ups of the dangers of smoking and even claims that smoking is good for us.

The bottom line: once I *accepted* the fact that news outlets exaggerate, and that people and even scientists are imperfect, I felt so much better because *I* said "No" to a bleak future. My mind rejects the idea of a bad future. I happily admit that news fasts are a joyful part of my life now.

I heard someone ask, "How can you be happy during a pandemic?" I love author Wayne Dyer's answer to a similar question in his PBS special *Seven Secrets to a Joyful Life.* (I also consider the late Dr. Dyer another one of my spiritual teachers, as I have read his books and attended his seminars). Dyer first posed some additional questions of his own. He asked, "How can I feel good when so much around me is bad? How can I feel good if my sister-in-law has cancer? How can I feel good if people on the other side of the planet are starving? How can I feel good if there are poor people and I have money?"

Dyer's advice was, "You cannot get sick enough to heal one person on this planet. You cannot get poor enough to make one person wealthy on this planet. You cannot get confused enough to unconfuse one person on this planet. No amount of you feeling bad is going to help anyone." The message again is *acceptance*. Thank you, Dr. Dyer.

When you wear the loose-fitting garment of acceptance every day, life feels better and more comfortable. You may notice your level of happiness and joy rises because you're not judging others. You experience less negativity. Sure, someone may say something or do something that you don't prefer, but it's OK because *you accept that everyone is on their own journey.*

Author Hawkins also pointed out that *acceptance* is the great healer of strife, conflict, and upset. (I love this sentence.) I'll say it again for you: acceptance is the great healer of strife, conflict, and upset.

I had a past situation where someone reneged on an agreement that we had, and I became very upset. But once I accepted it and let it go, it did not matter. Have you ever anticipated that something negative may happen, you get yourself all worked up, and then it doesn't happen? That choice seems like a waste of energy to me now, but it was a learning experience.

It's OK if we make a miscue, as long as we can learn something from it. I have heard Hawkins say mistakes can be more valuable than wins if you learn and grow from the experience.

Author Hawkins also stated, "In life, we will not understand all events and circumstances that happen, and that is OK. Acceptance is not passivity but non-positionality. The ego loves to take a position." I believe the attitude of acceptance helps control the ego, thus preventing the ego from controlling you.

Personally, adopting the attitude of acceptance has been positively liberating for me because negative emotions and negative thoughts are easily dismissed. The acceptance attitude has changed my life for the better.

Life lesson: allow yourself to *accept* the unfolding of life as it is. I teach my clients the Hawkins quote and how it changed my life.

The following ten "I statements" drive this point home:

1. I accept that we're all on our own journeys.
2. I accept we can always improve ourselves.
3. I accept responsibility to control my greatest power of choosing my thoughts.
4. I accept responsibility for my actions, my emotions, and my happiness.
5. I accept responsibility to have positive goals for myself.
6. I accept responsibility to laugh at myself and at life whenever the occasion arises.
7. I accept responsibility to let go of past transgressions.
8. I accept responsibility to be helpful to others.
9. I accept responsibility to take care of myself.
10. I accept responsibility to keep an attitude of gratitude.

As you use these statements or affirmations, notice they naturally strengthen your feeling of calm and personal development. They're also constant reminders of your greatest power.

Life's journey at some point will challenge you. *Accept the challenge*. Welcome it! See every sunrise as a new day. Exercising acceptance and optimizing your greatest power will keep you feeling happy and in good spirits as you're achieving your goals.

Keep in mind (as mentioned in chapter 2) that spiritual masters teach us the importance of focusing your intention on creating loving, positive, and compassionate thoughts. Why do they say this? Because the mind goes in the directions of these thoughts, which create a positive love vibration. That vibration radiates outward and brings love, joy, and happiness back to you! This positive, emitting energy helps everyone around you. Spiritual master David Hawkins proved that when you choose unconditional love all of humanity benefits.

As you continue to apply the mental strategies and the basic truths with your self-hypnosis goals, your confidence will soar. You'll be the master of your thoughts. This will attract all the happiness, love, and success you deserve.

Congratulations for acting and learning the three steps to help you achieve your goals and enjoy life. As I said earlier, just being presented with this material will automatically create an obvious positive effect.

Let's review the true headlines and important life-changing information you've learned:

- Your greatest power is your power to choose your thoughts.

- Always frame the two most important words "I am" in a positive light.

- The number one trait of your mind is that you go in the direction of your thoughts. So, keep positive and loving thoughts between your ears.

- What you hold in your mind tends to manifest, because what you think about, you bring about.

- Look at life from a positive point of view.

- Your subconscious mind is the home of your personal program.

- Have specific goals.

- The seven powerful mind techniques: affirmations; five-minute writing, printing, and speaking; "that's like me"; remove negative weeds; "I cancel that"; advertise to yourself; and seminar leader.

- The six subconscious change techniques: regression, anchor, anchor collapse, inner adviser, aversion, and posthypnotic suggestions.

- Self-hypnosis is the perfect tool to update your program for healthy habits, positive change, enhancement, relaxation, self-improvement, and feeling good about yourself. Spend time imagining positive future outcomes.

REVIEW OF MY TOP SIX LIFE LESSONS

1. Be open to change and new opportunities.

2. Make sure your language use is always positive and reflects what you truly want for yourself.

3. Accept the unfolding of life.

4. An attitude of gratitude is a winner (more on this in the bonus chapter).

5. Look for ways to laugh at life and yourself, because laughter is the best medicine (more on this in the bonus chapter).

6. When you want to do something, set a goal and do it (more on this in you know where: the bonus chapter).

Enjoy each day on your journey, with your new awareness and self-hypnosis skills. You'll continue to grow, improve, and evolve. You'll notice that the entire process seems comfortable, yielding happiness, joy, and success.

Please share this knowledge with your friends and loved ones.

Thank you for reading this book. I'm extremely grateful for your time and attention. I hope you see all the new possibilities for yourself. Enjoy your life, my friend. And please join me on social media. I always appreciate comments, questions, and advice. I wish you all the best!

In the next chapter, you'll find your self-hypnosis scripts, followed by the bonus chapter.

CHAPTER 12

FOUR SELF-HYPNOSIS SCRIPTS

YOU'RE NOW READY AND TOTALLY prepared for successful self-hypnosis. With a little practice recording, you will soon be a pro. This chapter contains four self-hypnosis scripts:

1. Total Relaxation
2. Finding Your Inner Adviser
3. Sleep Time
4. Being Funny

As mentioned previously, the initial step is to focus on your breathing and get into a relaxed and focused mental state. You may notice some slight variations of how each script addresses the relaxation process.

The first one is aptly called "Self-Hypnosis for Total Relaxation." I chose this script because many people seem to be stressed out with today's fast-paced lifestyle. This will be the perfect antidote.

The focus is on physically and mentally relaxing and allowing yourself to recharge. You'll feel refreshed afterward. I'd advise you to read through the script once or twice before making your recording. After you have some sessions under your belt and you feel ready, feel free to use some of the tools and techniques mentioned in earlier chapters to adapt the script to your specific goal. Or you may want to try it now and add whatever words feel right for you.

To begin, decide what time of day would be best to enter the self-hypnosis zone: before you go to sleep, when you first wake up, or at another time during the day. If you'd like to play the recording before bed, you can add statements like, "I will have a good night's sleep, and when I wake up tomorrow, I will feel refreshed and great."

Anything you see in parentheses is for direction only, not to verbalize aloud. When you see three dots after a word (like this: ...), it means "pause for a few seconds." As you continue to work and experiment, you'll find your own places to pause or add new words. It's OK to be creative and change any words as you like. If you're making a recording to use while going to sleep, include a lot of phrases like, "I will sleep deeply and calmly," "The body is ready for a good night's sleep," "I feel safe sleeping in my bed," or "When I wake up tomorrow, I will feel refreshed and ready to go."

Self-hypnosis audios always include a disclaimer, or warning, not to use while operating machinery or driving a car. (Well, since your eyes are closed during the session, obviously this is good advice.) Remember: slow and easy when you record. Have fun. You're going to love this!

SCRIPT #1
SELF-HYPNOSIS FOR TOTAL RELAXATION

Your recording starts here:

It's time for a relaxing self-hypnosis session. Put your cell phone on silent. Never use this while operating machinery or driving a car. Find a nice, comfortable place where you'll not be disturbed for the next twenty to twenty-five minutes. You can be sitting or lying down. Please have your arms by your sides and make sure your legs and ankles are not crossed so you can achieve good blood flow. It's time to relax and let go.

Before you begin, take a moment to physically tense the muscles in the body. Tense the arm muscles, tense the leg muscles. Squeeze your muscles for a few moments and make them feel tight…squeeze…good. Now take a great big deep breath through your nose, exhale through your nose, let the muscles release, let go and relax …

Inhale and exhale through your nose during the session. You'll be asked to use your imagination, or to repeat statements, or to nod your head. Please follow the suggestions to the best of your ability. If any other thoughts come into your mind, simply brush them aside and keep refocusing back on the session. You'll soon discover that by simply listening, you'll feel calm and relaxed.

There is no place you must go now; there's nothing you must do. Give yourself permission to relax and let go as you enjoy the feelings of calm and peace. You deserve it.

Please close your eyes and keep them closed until I ask you to open them. With your eyes closed now, imagine you're looking straight up, as if you're trying to look at your forehead. Rolling your eyes up into your forehead. Notice how the eyes feel in that upward position…

OK, now let your eyes relax, and let's take a few slow, deep breaths. Please take a nice big, slow deep breath in through your nose…hold one, two, three and let it come slowly out of your nose. Take another nice, deep inhalation…and let it come slowly out, noticing if you feel the air flow out of your nostrils, as you begin to let go and relax…This time, fill your lungs as deeply as you can, and hold your breath as deeply as you can, and hold your breath…hold, hold, hold, and let it out slowly and let go and relax, relax, relax…Every gentle breath helps you drift into deeper levels of relaxation.

Gently nod your head *yes, please.*

Anytime you nod your head during the session, you'll find this helps you feel more relaxed and confident. If you feel like moving or adjusting your position, that's fine. If you're not feeling any comfortable feelings yet that's OK, it will catch up to you.

Just hearing the following words now will help you feel calm and relaxed…Focus on the comfortable position that you're in… notice the body is gently sinking into that position…Imagine the muscles in the body are letting go and becoming soft and supple…it's as if the muscles are starting to sag…it's as if you're feeling like a loose, limp rag doll…

As you listen, begin to see yourself feeling calm and relaxed… calm and relaxed…calm and relaxed. Please focus your awareness on your eyes and eyelids. Please put your attention on your eyes and eyelids. Imagine your eyes feeling very sleepy and very tired. Imagine all the little, tiny muscles around your eyes are feeling heavy, sleepy, and tired…heavy, sleepy, and tired. Some people may experience a slight flutter around the eyes when they begin to relax—that's just a sign they're letting go…

Imagine it's one of those mornings when the alarm goes off and you feel like you didn't get enough sleep…you just feel so sleepy and so tired. You don't want to open your eyes because they feel soooo good being closed…It's as if it would be too much effort to even open your eyes…Of course, we know you could simply open them, but use your creative imagination to feel a comfortable, tired sensation around your eyes, so they feel heavy, sleepy, and tired…heavy, sleepy, and tired…They're perfectly comfortable being closed…

Create the sensation around your eyes, as if it would feel like too much effort to even open them, because they feel soooo good being closed…When you can create a sense of that feeling where your eyes feel so good being closed, and it will be too much effort to even open them, gently nod your head *yes, please…*

Very good. Anytime I ask you to nod your head, it will help you feel even more relaxed…now, allow that relaxed feeling around your eyelids to spread to the muscles in your face, allow your cheeks to relax…allow a little space between your teeth, allow your jaw to relax…

Imagine the muscles in your neck just letting go and relaxing, your shoulder muscles are becoming loose, limp, and relaxed… As you hear my voice, that helps you drift into a positive, relaxed, calm state…Imagine the muscles in your chest and stomach are letting go and relaxing…Imagine all the muscles in your back feel soft, supple, and relaxed…Imagine your hips are relaxing…Your thigh muscles are letting go and relaxing…your knees, calves, and ankles are relaxed…the muscles in your feet let go and relax, relax, relax…

You're beginning to feel a wonderful sense of relaxation. If this is true, gently nod your head *yes, please…*Very good, you're doing very well.

In a moment, I will count to the number three. When you hear the number three, you'll envision yourself standing at the top of a stairway. This will be the special stairway, the stairway of relaxation, with ten steps going down; the steps may even be numbered from ten to one. At the bottom of the stairs is a beautiful doorway. You'll hear a countdown from ten to one. With each number, step down to the next step. As you proceed down, allow each step to help you to drift into deeper levels of relaxation. Each step helps you sink into deeper levels of relaxation.

On the count of three, imagine yourself standing at the top of the stairway of relaxation…One, two, three…now imagine yourself standing at the top of the stairway. When you can imagine this, gently nod your head *yes, please*…Very good. Notice that there is a beautiful doorway at the bottom of the stairs. By the time you reach the bottom, you'll feel very, very relaxed.

Get ready for the initial step down. As the countdown starts, you may feel your foot hit the step. Here we go.

Number ten, stepping down, feeling more relaxed…

Nine, stepping down, feeling more relaxed…

Eight, stepping down, feeling more relaxed…

Seven, stepping down, feeling more deeply relaxed…

Six, stepping down, feeling more deeply relaxed…

As the body relaxes, the mind relaxes…

Five, stepping down, feeling more relaxed…

Four, stepping down, feeling more relaxed…

The more relaxed you feel, the better you feel…

Three, stepping down, feeling more relaxed…

Two, stepping down, feeling more relaxed…

One, stepping off, feeling very relaxed…

If you're feeling relaxed and calm, gently nod your head *yes, please*…very good. Now, before you there is a beautiful doorway. In a moment, we're going to go through the door. On the other side is a very special, safe place just for you, a place where you feel *very safe* and very comfortable in every way. Your safe place may be a room in your house, a place from your childhood, a place in nature, or a totally imaginary place like floating on a cloud. On the count of three, go through the door and discover your safe place. One...two...three...open the door and find yourself in your safe place...

When you're in that safe place, gently nod your head *yes, please*...Very good. Get nice and comfortable in your safe place, nice and comfortable. You'll remember where your safe place is. Let's go to an even deeper level of relaxation. I'm going to count down from ten to one. Every number you hear will bring you into a deeper level of relaxation.

Number ten, feeling more and more relaxed...going deeper down,

Nine, feeling more and more relaxed...going deeper down,

Eight, feeling more and more relaxed...going deeper down,

Seven, feeling more and more relaxed...going deeper down,

Six, feeling more and more relaxed...the more relaxed you feel, the better you feel,

Five, feeling more and more relaxed...as the body relaxes, the mind relaxes,

Four, feeling more and more relaxed....

Three, feeling more and more relaxed...

Two, feeling more and more relaxed...

One, feeling more and more relaxed...

The more relaxed you feel, the better you feel...If you're feeling peaceful and calm, gently nod your head *yes, please*...Very good...you're in your safe place; remember this feeling of your safe place.

Say the words out loud "I feel calm now." (pause)...

Repeat this phrase 3 times—"I feel calm now." (pause)...

Very good, let's save this positive, relaxing feeling and anchor it to your thumb and forefinger...Please use your nondominant hand and place your thumb and forefinger together. Place your thumb and forefinger together and gently press them and feel the wonderful feeling of relaxation and calm…as they're gently pressed together repeat three times, "I'm calm now," "I'm calm now," "I'm calm now."

(pause)

Very good. Let go of your fingers and let your hand rest. You've created a positive, powerful relaxation anchor. This positive, calm anchor can be used at any time to assist you to feel calm and at ease. By gently pressing your thumb and forefinger together, feeling calm and repeating the words, "I'm calm now," you'll instantly feel calm anywhere, anytime. And the beauty of it's that no one knows you're even doing it…

You'll now see how well it works. When I count to three, you'll imagine a scenario where in the past you may have felt some anxiety; but you'll use this positive anchor technique to immediately erase any tension and enjoy the feeling of being calm.

You'll imagine you're out somewhere, and something comes up that in the past may have produced some negative anxiety. Once you recognize the anxiety, you'll take a deep breath, let the safe place image come into your mind, and gently put your thumb and forefinger together. When you exhale, say, "I feel calm now," three times, and it will instantly eliminate and dissolve any anxious feelings.

Let's see how well it works. On the count of three, imagine you're in a situation that in the past may have caused anxiety. Then imagine you take a breath, let the safe place come into your mind, press your thumb and forefinger together, and say to yourself, "I'm calm now, I'm calm now, I'm calm now," and see how well it works…

I will count to three now and imagine it working for you. One, two, three…Very good. If you experienced the positive anchor working, nod your head *yes, please.*

Excellent.

Let go of your thumb and forefinger and let your hand relax now. Allow a feeling of gratitude to come over you for tapping into this calm feeling. What else are you thankful for in your life? Let's focus on that feeling of gratitude. Take a minute and focus on what or who you're thankful for.

(Give yourself time.)

The more relaxed you feel, the better you feel; as the body relaxes, the mind relaxes. This feeling of calm and peace you've created will get stronger as you use this audio recording. It's important for you to realize that you can relax. You've created this positive and powerful feeling of calmness and relaxation. Enjoy the positive feelings of relaxation.

This skill of relaxing is going to enhance the quality of your life. Schedule time for yourself every day to relax and let go of the outside world and enjoy the positive feelings of calmness totally and completely. Every time you use this audio, you'll relax deeper and deeper.

It's time for a repeat technique. Whatever you hear, simply repeat the words. You can say them out loud or say them silently to yourself; but allow the statements to be communicated to every level of your body, mind, and spirit.

I can relax...

I can relax...

I can relax...

I have a positive anchor for relaxing...

I have a positive anchor for relaxing...

I have a positive anchor for relaxing...

I take time for myself to relax...

I take time for myself to relax...

I take time for myself to relax...

I confidently relax whenever I choose.

I confidently relax whenever I choose.

I confidently relax whenever I choose.

I enjoy feeling relaxed…

I enjoy feeling relaxed…

I enjoy feeling relaxed…

If I need to calm myself, I can easily do it

If I need to calm myself, I can easily do it

If I need to calm myself, I can easily do it

I can do it.

I can do it.

I can do it.

I see myself taking the time for myself to relax…

I see myself taking the time for myself to relax…

I see myself taking the time for myself to relax…

I confidently relax whenever I choose.

I confidently relax whenever I choose.

I confidently relax whenever I choose.

I like my calm and confident feelings.

I like my calm and confident feelings.

I like my calm and confident feelings.

Very good. Gently press your thumb and forefinger together and repeat, "I'm relaxed now," three times as you gently press your thumb and forefinger together. Do it now. This technique erases any anxious feelings which may come up. It's a simple and powerful technique that you can use anytime, and no one will even know that you're doing it.

Very good. When I count to three…imagine it's a couple of days from now, and you may notice an anxious feeling. When you do, see yourself take a deep breath; imagine your safe place and gently press your thumb and forefinger together and repeat a few times, "I'm relaxed now." Any anxious thought disappears into a calm, confident feeling. It's as if you just erased it. One, two, three…imagine it's two days from now, and pretend you have an anxious feeling, take a deep breath, imagine your safe place, put your thumb and forefinger together, and say, "I'm relaxed now," "I'm relaxed now," "I'm relaxed now," and notice you erase any anxious feelings.

As time goes on, you'll need this technique less and less, because you simply will be a calm person all the time. You'll look calm, you will feel calm, and you will act calm.

We will be ending this session in a moment, and when it's over, you'll feel like you had a wonderful, relaxing, and rejuvenating nap. You accept the fact that you have inner power to focus and create whatever you want for yourself. Stay positive; you're a positive person. And the next time you use this session you'll notice how easily you glide into the focused mental state known as self-hypnosis.

(Start to put a lot more energy back into your voice.) In a moment, I'm going to count to five, and when I get to the number five, you'll feel wide awake and alert. You'll feel like you just had a good nap! (Speak louder here.) One…starting to come up, two… coming up more and more, three…let energy come back into the body, four…start to move your body. When you open your eyes, you'll feel calm and alert. Five…eyes open, wide awake and alert and feeling great! Wide awake, alert and feeling positive and calm! (End recording here.)

***

Congratulations on working through self-hypnosis for total re-laxation! You did it!

You can use this script as a basis for any goal. The knowledge you've gained from reading this book will help you adjust the words to match what you want to achieve and to focus on.

SCRIPT #2
YOUR INNER ADVISER

What's an *inner adviser*? This amazing program helps you receive answers to your questions. Have you ever had a situation
where you were not 100 percent clear on a decision? You were
not sure what to do? This technique may be very insightful to
clarifying information.

Your recording starts here:

It's time for a relaxing self-hypnosis session. Put your cell phone
on silent. Don't use this process while operating machinery or
driving a car. Find a nice, comfortable place where you'll not be
disturbed for the next twenty-five minutes. You can be sitting or
lying down. Please have your arms by your sides and make sure
your legs and ankles are not crossed so you can achieve good
blood flow. It's time to relax and let go.

Before you begin, take a moment to physically tense the muscles
in the body. Tense the arm muscles, tense the leg muscles.
Squeeze your muscles for a few moments and make them feel
tight...squeeze...good. Now take a great big deep breath in
through your nose, exhale, let the muscles release, let go and
relax...

Inhale and exhale through your nose during the session. You'll
be asked to use your imagination, to repeat statements, or to
nod your head. Please follow the suggestions to the best of your
ability. If any other thoughts come into your mind, simply brush
them aside and keep refocusing back on the session. You'll soon
discover that by simply listening, you'll feel calm and relaxed.

There is no place you must go now; there's nothing you must
do. Give yourself permission to relax and let go as you enjoy the
feelings of calm and peace. You deserve it.

Please close your eyes and keep them closed until I ask you to open them. With your eyes closed now, imagine you're looking straight up, as if you're trying to look at your forehead. Rolling your eyes up into your forehead, notice how the eyes feel in that upward position...

OK, now let your eyes relax, and let's take a few slow, deep breaths. Please take a nice big, slow deep breath in through your nose...and let it come slowly out of your mouth, feeling the air as it passes between your lips...Take another nice, deep inhalation...and let it come slowly out of your nose, feeling the breath pass between your nostrils as you begin to let go and relax...This time, fill your lungs as deeply as you can, and hold your breath, as deeply as you can and hold your breath...hold, hold, hold, and let it out slowly and let go and relax, relax, relax...Every gentle breath helps you drift into deeper levels of relaxation. Anytime I ask you to nod your head, you'll find this also helps you feel more relaxed. If you feel like moving or adjusting your position, that's fine.

Hearing my voice now simply helps you feel calm and relaxed... Focus on the comfortable position that you're in...notice the body is gently sinking into that position...Imagine the muscles in the body are letting go and becoming soft and supple...it's as if the muscles are starting to sag...it's as if you're feeling like a loose limp, rag doll...It's OK if you're not noticing all the relaxed feelings yet; they'll catch up to you.

As you listen, begin to see yourself feeling calm and relaxed... calm and relaxed...calm and relaxed. Please focus your awareness on your eyes and eyelids. Put your attention on your eyes and eyelids. Imagine your eyes feeling very sleepy and very tired. Imagine all the little, tiny muscles around your eyes are feeling heavy, sleepy, and tired...heavy, sleepy, and tired. Some people may experience a slight flutter around the eyes when they begin to relax—that's just a sign they're letting go...

Imagine it's one of those mornings when the alarm goes off and you feel like you didn't get enough sleep...you just feel so sleepy and so tired. You don't want to open your eyes because they feel soooo good being closed...It's as if it would be too much effort to even open your eyes...Of course, we know you could simply open them, but use your creative imagination to feel a comfortable, tired sensation around your eyes, so they feel heavy, sleepy, and tired...heavy, sleepy, and tired...They're perfectly comfortable being closed...

Create the sensation around your eyes, as if it would feel like too much effort to even open them, because they feel soooo good being closed...When you can create a sense of that feeling where your eyes feel so good being closed, and it will be too much effort to even open them, gently nod your head *yes, please*...

Very good. Anytime I ask you to gently nod your head, it will help you feel even more relaxed...now, allow that relaxed feeling around your eyelids to spread to the muscles in your face, allow your cheeks to relax...allow a little space between your teeth, allow your jaw to relax...

Imagine the muscles in your neck just letting go and relaxing, your shoulder muscles are becoming loose, limp, and relaxed... simply listening now helps you drift into a positive, relaxed, calm state...Imagine the muscles in your chest and stomach are letting go and relaxing...Imagine all the muscles in your back feel soft, supple, and relaxed...Imagine your hips are relaxing... Your thigh muscles are letting go and relaxing...your knees, calves, and ankles are relaxed...the muscles in your feet let go and relax, relax, relax...

You're beginning to feel a wonderful sense of relaxation. If this is true, gently nod your head *yes, please*... Very good, you're doing very well.

In a moment I will count to the number three. When you hear the number three, you'll envision yourself standing at the top of a stairway. This will be the special stairway, the stairway of relaxation, with ten steps going down; the steps may even be numbered from ten to one. At the bottom of the stairs is a beautiful doorway. You'll hear a count down from ten to one. With each number, step down to the next step. As you proceed down you will drift into deeper levels of relaxation, as if each step slowly brings you into deeper levels of relaxation.

On the count of three, imagine yourself standing at the top of the stairway of relaxation...One, two, three...Imagine yourself standing at the top of the stairway. When you can imagine this, gently nod your head *yes, please*...Very good. Notice that there is a beautiful doorway at the bottom of the stairs. By the time you reach the bottom, you'll feel very, very relaxed.

Get ready for the initial step. As the countdown starts, you may feel your foot hit the step. Here we go.

Number ten, stepping down, feeling more relaxed...

Nine, stepping down, feeling more relaxed...

Eight, stepping down, feeling more relaxed...

Seven, stepping down, feeling more relaxed...

Six, stepping down, feeling more relaxed...

As the body relaxes, the mind relaxes...

Five, stepping down, feeling more relaxed...

Four, stepping down, feeling more relaxed...

The more relaxed you feel, the better you feel...

Three, stepping down, feeling more relaxed...

Two, stepping down, feeling more relaxed...

One, stepping off, feeling very relaxed...

If you're feeling relaxed and calm, gently nod your head *yes, please*...Very good. Now, before you there is a beautiful doorway. In a moment, we're going to go through the door. On the other side is a very special, safe place just for you, a place where you feel *very safe* and very comfortable in every way. Your safe place may be a room in your house, or a place from your childhood, a place in nature, or a totally imaginary place like floating on a cloud. On the count of three, go through the door and discover your safe place. One...two...three...open the door and discover yourself in your safe place...

When you're in that safe place, gently nod your head *yes, please*...Very good. Get nice and comfortable in your safe place, nice and comfortable. You'll remember where your safe place is. Let's go to an even deeper level of relaxation. You will hear a count down from ten to one. Every number you hear will bring you into to a deeper level of relaxation.

Number ten, feeling more and more relaxed...going deeper down,

Nine, feeling more and more relaxed...going deeper down,

Eight, feeling more and more relaxed...going deeper down,

Seven, feeling more and more relaxed...going deeper down,

Six, feeling more and more relaxed...the more relaxed you feel, the better you feel,

Five, feeling more and more relaxed...as the body relaxes, the mind relaxes.

Four, feeling more and more relaxed....

Three, feeling more and more relaxed...

Two, feeling more and more relaxed...

One, feeling more and more relaxed...

The more relaxed you feel, the better you feel...If you're feeling peaceful and calm, gently nod your head *yes, please*...Very good...you're in your safe place; You'll remember your safe place.

Please repeat this phrase three times: "I feel calm now," do it now...(pause)...

The more relaxed you feel, the better you feel; as the body relaxes, the mind relaxes. This feeling of calm and peace will continue as you're listening.

In a moment, we will count back from five to the number one. Let's go back into your memory bank for a positive memory. Positive memories are fun. Maybe it was something that happened yesterday or something that happened many years ago. But let's bring back a happy positive vibration where you felt very good about it. Going to count back now listen closely, and by the time we get to the number one, hey, happy-confident, good-feeling memory will come in to your mind. Five going back back back, four going back to a happy, positive memory, three back back back, I was feeling good and, two let a positive memory to come into your mind, and one let a positive memory come into your mind...

When you have a positive memory just gently nod your head, please...

Very good, focus on the positive feelings in this positive memory.

Let that fade away, and just relax, relax, relax. Feeling safe and calm...

Feeling safe and calm...

Imagine that you're sitting on a beautiful beach. There is no one else here but you. It's perfect weather for you, sunny and nice. You're very comfortable as you sit on a blanket facing the ocean. It's a clear, sunny day with a beautiful, blue sky. You may feel a slight breeze as you hear the gentle waves lapping back and forth. It's peaceful.

As you're enjoying the environment and your solitude, you sense there is a reason to be here at this moment. You've been wondering about something. Maybe you're searching for advice or clarity. You feel totally calm and at peace. Off in the distance, you notice a figure walking along on the beach coming your way. You're feeling a quiet confidence about yourself as you sit here. The figure slowly gets closer. You're open and receptive. You feel open to suggestions or advice.

Notice again how calm and safe you feel. As you look, the image is getting closer and closer. The person emanates a sense of love and security and is now only steps away. It may be someone you recognize, or it may not. Perhaps it's just a helpful being. The person gently approaches you, radiating love and acceptance. Love and acceptance. You know they're here for you. They come right up to you now, but they don't talk or verbalize anything. They radiate unconditional love and acceptance. You feel like you can read each other's minds. As crystal clear as can be, you sense them saying, "Ask, please ask me."

You understand they're here for you, now ask whatever you wish. The answer may be instantaneous, or it may take some time. It may be a sign or a symbol or something as direct as a one-on-one conversation. Ask your question.

(Pause for a minute or so.)

When you have your answer, you may ask a follow-up question, or just express the feeling of gratitude for the information. (Pause for a minute or so.)

They send love as they slowly begin to walk away. You extend gratitude as the figure slowly continues walking down the beach. You feel wonderful. You feel calm. The figure slowly disappears.

You have new insight now, as you calmly relax.

We will be ending the session in a moment, and when it's over, you'll feel like you had a wonderful, relaxing, and rejuvenating nap. And now you have new information, which feels good. And the next time you use this session you'll notice how easily you glide into the focused mental state known as self-hypnosis.

(Start to put a lot more energy back into your voice.) In a moment, you'll hear the count one to five, and at the number five, you'll feel wide awake and alert. You'll feel like you just had a good nap! (Speak louder here.) One…starting to come up, two… coming up more and more, three…let energy come back into the body, four…start to move your body. When you open your eyes, you'll feel calm and alert. Five…eyes open, wide awake, alert, and feeling great! Wide awake, alert, and feeling positive and calm! (End recording here.)

**

Congratulations on experiencing the inner adviser! You did it!

SCRIPT #3
GOOD NIGHT'S SLEEP

What's there's no debate about how important a good night's sleep is for overall health and well-being, as I mentioned earlier in the book, good sleep hygiene is fundamentally important for you to take control of your health. The basic formula includes no screens two to three hours before bed and no food three to four hours before bed. Your bedroom should be dark (no lights), and on the cool side is perfect for a good night's sleep. The sleep experts always say our beds should be for sleeping and sex, and that's it.

When you're recording this, obviously, you want to speak in very relaxed, low hushed tones, and toward the end, you can speak really low and barely whisper.

Your recording starts here:

OK, it's time for a great night's sleep and first thing you need to do is get yourself in a nice relaxed comfortable position so take a moment now and do that, please…

I'd like you to place your attention on how your body is lying on the mattress, focus on where the body meets the mattress and how the body is gently sinking into that position, and the muscles are just starting to sag and relax. Take a great big deep breath in through your nose as deeply as you can and hold it, and take a second breath in and hold it…now let it out nice and slowly. Let's take some time to focus on gratitude and what we have to be thankful about, which may include: "I'm still alive," "I have a roof over my head," or any person in your life you may be thankful for, or anything you may have enjoyed like a nice sunny day, and so on.

(Pause for a minute or so as you recognize what to be grateful for.)

You're going to sleep so deeply tonight, and when you awake in the morning, you'll feel very good.

Simply listening to the words now helps you feel calm and relaxed. Imagine the muscles in the body are letting go and becoming soft and supple.

OK, now let your eyes relax, and let's take a few slow, deep breaths. Please take a nice big, slow deep breath in through your nose...and let it come slowly out of your nose, feeling the air as it passes between your nostrils...Take another nice, deep inhalation...and let it come slowly out of your nose feeling the breath pass between your nostrils as you begin to let go and relax...This time, fill your lungs as deeply as you can, and hold your breath, as deeply as you can and hold your breath...hold, hold, hold, and let it out slowly and let go and relax, relax, relax...Every gentle breath helps you drift into deeper levels of relaxation. Anytime I ask you to nod your head, you'll find this also helps you feel more relaxed.

Now, focus on where the body meets the mattress and how the muscles are gently sinking into that position, and it feels safe and comfortable. Take a great big deep breath now in through your nose is deeply as you can and let it out nice and slowly. Imagine the body just gently sinks into that position and your muscles just relax.

Focus your awareness on your eyes and eyelids, and just imagine that your eyes and eyelids are very heavy, sleepy, and tired. Imagine the eyelids, feel heavy, sleepy, and tired. Just pretend that your eyes and eyelids are so sleepy and tired, it feels like it was one of those mornings where the alarm went off and it felt like you didn't get enough sleep. To the best of your ability create that feeling around your eyes and eyelids where they feel heavy, sleepy, and tired, heavy, sleepy, and tired. Very good.

Imagine that relaxed feeling spreading to the muscles in your face and the muscles in your cheeks and allow your jaw to relax, allow a little space between your teeth. Imagine the neck, muscles, and shoulder muscles just let go and relax and imagine the muscles in your chest and arms and wrists and hands. Just start to feel loose, limp, and relaxed. Loose, limp, and relaxed. Now imagine the muscles in your hips and legs just feel so comfortable and so relaxed, so comfortable and so relaxed, the muscles in your ankles and feet just feel so comfortable and relaxed.

And if you're feeling safe and comfortable, gently nod your head *yes, please…*

In a moment I will count to the number three. When you hear the number three, you'll envision yourself standing at the top of a very special stairway, the stairway of sleep and rest. This special stairway of sleep and rest will have ten steps going down; the steps may even be numbered from ten to one. At the bottom of the stairs is a beautiful doorway. You'll hear a count down from ten to one. With each number, step down to the next step. As you proceed down you will sink into deeper levels of relaxation as you begin to drift into a safe night's sleep.

On the count of three, imagine yourself standing at the top of the stairway of sleep…One, two, three…Imagine yourself now standing at the top of the stairway. When you can imagine this, gently nod your head *yes, please…*Very good. Notice that there is a beautiful doorway at the bottom of the stairs. By the time you reach the bottom, you'll feel very, very sleepy and relaxed. Get ready for the initial step you may actually feel your foot hit the step.

Here we go, number ten, stepping down feeling more relaxed…

Number nine, stepping down feeling more relaxed and sleepier…

Number eight, stepping down feeling more relaxed and sleepier…

Number seven, stepping down feeling more relaxed and sleepier…

Number six, stepping down feeling more relaxed and sleepier…

Number five, stepping down feeling more relaxed and sleepier…

Number four, stepping down feeling more relaxed and sleepier...

Number three, stepping down feeling more and more relaxed and sleepier...

Number two, stepping down feeling more and more relaxed and sleepier...

Number one, stepping down feeling more and more relaxed and sleepier.

Very good, on the count of three we will go through the doorway, and you will discover a place where you feel very safe in every way. Most people choose their bedroom for a safe place, but you may imagine any place you would like, it could be a place in nature, or it could be a place from your childhood, on the count of three, let's open the door and discover your safe place. One, two, three...

Now you are in your safe place, listen to a slow count down from ten to one and you will notice that you are sinking deeper and deeper into a peaceful night's sleep...

Here we go, number ten, stepping down feeling more relaxed...

Number nine, stepping down calmly drifting into a restful night's sleep...

Number eight, stepping down feeling more relaxed and sleepier...

Number seven, stepping down feeling more relaxed and sleepier...

Number six, stepping down feeling more relaxed and sleepier...

Number five, stepping down feeling more relaxed and sleepier...

Number four, stepping down feeling more relaxed and sleepier...

Number three, stepping down feeling more and more relaxed and sleepier...

Number two, stepping down feeling more and more relaxed and sleepier...

Number one, stepping down feeling more and more relaxed and sleepier.

(Start talking very softly now)

You're becoming a confident sleeper as you drift off feeling at peace and calm.

You're becoming a confident sleeper as you drift off feeling at peace and calm.

You are a sound sleeper, and you think of yourself as a good sleeper.

You will hear a countdown from five to one. This time, imagine every number helps you feel twice as relaxed and twice as sleepy.

Number five feeling twice as sleepy.

Number four feeling twice as sleepy.

Number three feeling twice as sleepy.

Number two feeling twice as sleepy.

Number one feeling twice as sleepy

You feel so good, and you are a good sleeper, you are a confident sleeper.

You love to sleep. You enjoy sleeping. You are a good sleeper. You take care of your health.

You make healthy choices for yourself.

You enjoy feeling more confident about yourself and about life; you keep a positive attitude about yourself, as you drift into a safe deep sleep. You enjoy sleeping like this, so deeply relaxed and so peaceful. You focus on positive expectations for yourself. You understand everything is unfolding as it should. You're feeling the acceptance of life. You enjoy feeling confident with yourself and your life. You enjoy life's simple pleasures. You appreciate yourself and others in your life more than ever.

You enjoy sleeping like this, so deeply, so relaxed, so peaceful.

(Speak very sleepier softly for this one) Feeling much sleepier, relaxed, and very good as you drift off into a very safe night's sleep.

Good night.

Good night.

Good night.

Good night.

SCRIPT #4
BEING FUNNIER AND LAUGHING MORE

So, you would like to be funnier? Then this script is for you.

Your recording starts here:

It's time for a relaxing self-hypnosis session to learn how to be funnier and how to get more laughs. Put your cell phone on silent. This process is for relaxation and never while operating machinery or driving a car. Find a nice, comfortable place where you'll not be disturbed for the next twenty-five minutes. You can be sitting or lying down. Please have your arms by your sides and make sure your legs and ankles are not crossed so you can achieve good blood flow. It's time to relax and let go.

Before you begin, take a moment to physically tense the muscles in the body. Tense the arm muscles, tense the leg muscles. Squeeze your muscles for a few moments and make them feel tight…squeeze…good. Now take a great big deep breath in through your nose, exhale, let the muscles release, let go and relax…

Please inhale and exhale through your nose during the session. You'll be asked to use your imagination, to repeat statements, or to nod your head. Please follow the suggestions to the best of your ability. If any other thoughts come into your mind, simply brush them aside and keep refocusing back on the session. You'll soon discover that by simply listening, you'll feel calm and relaxed.

There is no place you must go now; there's nothing you must do. Give yourself permission to relax and let go as you enjoy the feelings of calm and peace. You deserve it.

Please close your eyes and keep them closed until I ask you to open them. With your eyes closed now, imagine you're looking straight up, as if you're trying to look at your forehead. Rolling your eyes up into your forehead, notice how the eyes feel in that upward position...

OK, now let your eyes relax, and let's take a few slow, deep breaths. Please take a nice. big, slow deep breath in through your nose...and let it come slowly out of your nose feeling the air as it passes between your nostrils...Take another nice, deep inhalation...and let it come slowly out, feeling as you begin to let go and relax...This time, fill your lungs as deeply as you can, and hold your breath, as deeply as you can, and hold your breath... hold, hold, hold, and let it out slowly and let go and relax, relax, relax...Every gentle breath helps you drift into deeper levels of relaxation. Gently nod your head *yes, please*... Anytime I ask you to nod your head, you'll find this also helps you feel more relaxed. If you feel like moving or adjusting your position, that's fine.

Listening now simply helps you feel calm and relaxed...Focus on the comfortable position that you're in...notice the body is gently sinking into that position...Imagine the muscles in the body are letting go and becoming soft and supple...it's as if the muscles are starting to sag...it's as if you're feeling like a loose, limp rag doll...It's OK if you're not noticing all the relaxed feelings yet; they'll catch up to you.

As you hear these words, begin to see yourself feeling calm and relaxed...calm and relaxed...calm and relaxed. Please focus your awareness on your eyes and eyelids. Put your attention on your eyes and eyelids. Imagine your eyes feeling very sleepy and very tired. Imagine all the little, tiny muscles around your eyes are feeling heavy, sleepy, and tired...heavy, sleepy, and tired. Some people may experience a slight flutter around the eyes when they begin to relax—that's just a sign they're letting go...

Imagine it's one of those mornings when the alarm goes off and you feel like you didn't get enough sleep...you just feel so sleepy and so tired. You don't want to open your eyes because they feel soooo good being closed...It's as if it would be too much effort to even open your eyes...Of course, we know you could simply

open them, but use your creative imagination to feel a comfortable, tired sensation around your eyes, so they feel heavy, sleepy,
and tired…heavy, sleepy, and tired…They're perfectly comfortable being closed…

Create the sensation around your eyes, as if it would feel like too
much effort to even open them, because they feel soooo good
being closed… Create a sense of feeling where your eyes feel
so good being closed, and it will feel like it is too much effort to
even open them… Yes, the eyes love being closed now, if that is
true gently nod your head *yes, please*…

Very good. Anytime I ask you to nod your head, it will help you
feel even more relaxed…now, allow that relaxed feeling around
your eyelids to spread to the muscles in your face, allow your
cheeks to relax…allow a little space between your teeth, allow
your jaw to relax…

Imagine the muscles in your neck just letting go and relaxing,
your shoulder muscles are becoming loose, limp, and relaxed…
As you hear my voice, that helps you drift into a positive, relaxed, calm state…Imagine the muscles in your chest and
stomach are letting go and relaxing…Imagine all the muscles in
your back feel soft, supple, and relaxed…Imagine your hips are
relaxing…Your thigh muscles are letting go and relaxing…your
knees, calves, and ankles are relaxed…the muscles in your feet
let go and relax, relax, relax…

You're beginning to feel a wonderful sense of relaxation in self-
hypnosis and if this is true, gently nod your head *yes, please*…
Very good, you're doing very well.

In a moment, I will count to the number three. When you hear
the number three, you'll envision yourself standing at the top
of a stairway. This will be the special stairway, the stairway of
relaxation, with ten steps going down; the steps may even be
numbered from ten to one. At the bottom of the stairs is a beautiful doorway. You'll hear a count down from ten to one. With

each number, step down to the next step. As you proceed down, drift into deeper levels of relaxation.

On the count of three, imagine yourself standing at the top of the stairway of relaxation...One, two, three...Imagine yourself standing at the top of the stairway. When you can imagine this, gently nod your head *yes, please*...Very good. Notice that there is a beautiful doorway at the bottom of the stairs. By the time you reach the bottom, you'll feel very, very relaxed.

Get ready for the initial step. As the countdown starts, you may feel your foot hit the step. Here we go.

Number ten, stepping down, feeling more relaxed...

Nine, stepping down, feeling more relaxed...

Eight, stepping down, feeling more relaxed...

Seven, stepping down, feeling more relaxed...

Six, stepping down, feeling more relaxed...

As the body relaxes, the mind relaxes...

Five, stepping down, feeling more relaxed...

Four, stepping down, feeling more relaxed...

The more relaxed you feel, the better you feel...

Three, stepping down, feeling more relaxed...

Two, stepping down, feeling more relaxed...

One, stepping off, feeling very relaxed...

If you're feeling relaxed and calm, gently nod your head *yes, please*...Very good. Now, before you there is a beautiful doorway. In a moment, we're going to go through the door. On the other side is a very special safe place just for you, a place where you feel *very safe* and very comfortable in every way. Your safe place may be a room in your house, or a place from your childhood, a place in nature, or a totally imaginary place like floating on a cloud. On the count of three, go through the door and discover your safe place. One…two…three…open the door and find yourself in your safe place…

When you're in that safe place, gently nod your head *yes, please*…Very good. Get nice and comfortable in your safe place, nice and comfortable. You'll remember where your safe place is. Let's go to an even deeper level of relaxation. I'm going to count down from ten to one. Every number you hear will bring you into a deeper level of relaxation.

Number ten, feeling more and more relaxed…going deeper down,

Nine, feeling more and more relaxed…going deeper down,

Eight, feeling more and more relaxed…going deeper down,

Seven, feeling more and more relaxed…going deeper down,

Six, feeling more and more relaxed…the more relaxed you feel, the better you feel,

Five, feeling more and more relaxed…as the body relaxes, the mind relaxes.

Four, feeling more and more relaxed….

Three, feeling more and more relaxed…

Two, feeling more and more relaxed…

One, feeling more and more relaxed…

The more relaxed you feel, the better you feel…If you're feel-ing peaceful and calm, gently nod your head *yes, please*…Very good…you're in your safe place. You'll remember your safe place. Experiencing this level of calm is very good for you.

Repeat this phrase three times: "I feel calm now." Do it now… (pause)…

The more relaxed you feel, the better you feel; as the body relaxes, the mind relaxes. This feeling of calm and peace will continue as you're listening.

I'm going to count down from five to one, when you hear the number one allow a positive memory to come into your mind, something that you did on your own that you like, something you did on your own that made you feel positive. It could be an old school memory where you got an A on a test, a sports memory, or maybe you helped someone and that gave you a positive feeling, or maybe you were just enjoying a laughing fit. Counting back to a positive, feel-good memory five, four, three, two, and one allows a positive memory to come into your mind. When it does, just nod your head *yes, please*. Enjoy the feelings of this positive event…imagine the feelings doubling.

Take a slow, deep breath and relax and just enjoy the calm feeling.

In a moment, I'm going to count back from five to one. I'd like you to go back into your memory bank for something that made you laugh, oh it was soooo funny. You were laughing out loud. Let's see what comes up. I'm counting back now, let a good funny memory come into your mind, counting back, five going back to a funny time, four back, back, back, three, I was laughing so hard, two back, and one, let a funny memory come into your mind, and feel free to laugh now about it…it was funny…. Enjoy the wonderful feelings of laughter!

…

Let that fade away…

Let that fade away…and let's do that again, we will go to another time you were laughing at something, I'm counting back now, let a good funny memory come into your mind, counting back, five going back to a funny time, four back, back, back, three, I was laughing so hard, two back, and one, let a funny memory come into your mind, and feel free to laugh now about it…it was funny…. Enjoy the wonderful feelings of laughter!

Very good, this time, I'd like you to let one of your favorite comedians come into your mind, I'll count to the number three and allow one of your favorite comedians to come into your mind. Here we go…one, two, and three…let one of your favorite comedians come into your mind. See them being funny…and repeat to yourself, "That is like me. That's like me. That's like me…"

Relax, relax, relax…

Think of someone who you think is funny, maybe someone you know personally or someone in the public eye. Let the person come into your mind. Now imagine you're standing right next to them shoulder to shoulder. You'll hear a count from one to three, this time on the number three, you magically merge your image in with theirs, and you'll be looking out through their eyes, listening through their ears, and feeling their confidence of guiding people to see the funny, guiding people to feel the laughter. One, two, and three…merge the images…and look out through their eyes and feel the confidence of knowing what's funny. And enjoying the laughter it creates…

On the count of three this time, unmerge but keep the feelings of confidence and the funny with you, keep the confidence and the funny with you! Let that fade away and relax. And relax, relax, relax.

It's time for a repeat technique. Whatever you hear, simply repeat the words. You can say them out loud or say them silently to yourself; but allow the statements to be communicated to every level of your body, mind, and spirit.

I can be funny…

I can be funny…

I can be funny…

I can relax…

I can relax…

I can relax…

I have the ability to see the humor in every situation…

I have the ability to see the humor in every situation…

I have the ability to see the humor in every situation...
I know how to be funny...
I know how to be funny...
I know how to be funny...
I love to laugh and make people laugh...
I love to laugh and make people laugh...
I love to laugh and make people laugh...
People notice I'm funny...
People notice I'm funny...
People notice I'm funny...
I enjoy improving my comedy writing...
I enjoy improving my comedy writing...
I enjoy improving my comedy writing...
I have fun creating comedy...
I have fun creating comedy...
I have fun creating comedy...
I am thankful for laughter...
I am thankful for laughter...
I am thankful for laughter...
Laughter is a beautiful sound...
Laughter is a beautiful sound...
Laughter is a beautiful sound...
It's a positive experience when you laugh...
It's a positive experience when you laugh...
It's a positive experience when you laugh...
I love to laugh and make people laugh...
I love to laugh and make people laugh...

I love to laugh and make people laugh…

And relax, relax, relax, relax…

In a moment, you'll hear a count to the number three. This time, you'll imagine yourself in front of others being funny, see yourself having fun as you say and do things that make everyone laugh and have fun.

Here we go, one, two, and three…

Imagine yourself in front of others being funny, maybe you're in a social situation or maybe you're on stage…

See yourself having fun as you say and do things that make everyone laugh and have fun. And it feels good…

We will be ending the session in a moment, and when it's over, you'll feel like you had a wonderful, relaxing, and rejuvenating nap. And feel like you're a funny person who can guide people into laughter. And the next time you use this session, you'll notice how easily you glide into the focused mental state known as self-hypnosis.

(Start to put a lot more energy back into your voice.) In a moment, you'll hear the count one to five, and at the number five, you'll feel wide awake and alert. You'll feel like you just had a good nap! (Speak louder here.) One…starting to come up, two…coming up more and more, three…let energy come back into the body, four…start to move your body. When you open your eyes, you'll feel calm and alert. Five…eyes open, wide awake, alert, and feeling great! Wide awake, alert, and feeling positive and calm!

(End recording here.)

ABOUT THE AUTHOR

FROM TURKEY FARMER TO OPERATING ROOM WORKER TO TEACHER TO COMEDIAN TO DOCTOR OF HYPNOTHERAPY

WHEN YOU COME TO A FORK IN THE ROAD, TAKE IT.
—YOGI BERRA

I'D LIKE TO SHARE SOME of the lessons from my journey through life and how I arrived at being a hypnotherapist. I hope this chapter will be helpful, entertaining, and informative. I grew up in Bucks County, Pennsylvania, a northern suburb of Philadelphia. After graduating from Neshaminy High School in 1971, I was not sure what type of full-time work would suit me, but I knew I wanted to stay busy. At that time my goal was just to work. I loved to work, because everyone in my family worked. No one ever complained about their job. The four-letter word you would *never* want to be called in our family was *lazy*.

All four of my grandparents immigrated from Italy to the United States in the 1920s. If you contrast the opportunities available to them in Italy to the United States, it's a night and day difference, like comparing Frankenstein to Brad Pitt. Their journey to a new country represents two important **life lessons:** first, be open to risk, change, and opportunity; and second, an attitude of gratitude is a positive force for good. My heart is full of gratitude for their courageous decision to make the trip to the United States. My mom told me that the most excited, happiest, and grateful she had ever seen my grandfather was the day he became a US citizen.

My family's work ethic and acceptance of responsibility and accountability was a great message and a positive force for me. As a youngster I could not wait to get a job and be like the rest of the men in my family. I am so grateful for my family.

JOBS AND MORE JOBS

My first full-time job was a summer gig, at age fourteen. I made eighty cents an hour at Styer's fruit farm in Langhorne, Pennsylvania. Twenty-five years later, when I told my children about it, they said, "Only eighty cents an hour? That just shows how old you are, Dad."

The following summer, at age fifteen, I had a specific goal: I needed to raise $300 for car insurance before I turned sixteen. My full-time job that summer was on a turkey farm earning $1.25 an hour. For a kid in 1968, that was a lot of bucks. There was one aspect of turkey farm labor that really made me laugh. I'm talking about artificial insemination of the hens, which the farmers do because it helps the hens lay more eggs. The process involves collecting sperm from the males ("toms") and injecting it into the hens. Oh, such fun!

How do you collect sperm from a male turkey, you ask? With sensual massage, of course, or, as we jokingly called it, jerking off a turkey. (And you thought *your* job was crazy). I was not the one to "turn on" the turkeys. No, that was the responsibility of the farm foreman, Bill, a balding man in his mid-fifties. He was always sporting a scruffy beard, dirty T-shirt, and a cigar hanging out of his mouth. One of us had to hold the Tom, while Bill would cup his hand and slied under the bird, and rub and rub, and soon the turkey would happily ejaculate. I liked Bill; but the male Toms LOVED HIM!

After about one hundred of these male turkeys had their fun, we would then go to the hen house and be joined by other workers. We would cordon off a section with portable fencing. Another guy and I had to grab the hens, pick them up, put them on a box, and hold them down while Bill poked his big syringe into their back side and squirted some of the "good stuff" in there. We would do this all day long. Imagine catching a female turkey on a hot, sticky, humid, summer day, carrying it with wings a-flappin', dust a-flyin', feathers a-floatin', and holding it down on a box while a smelly old farmer jabbed its vagina with a syringe full of turkey spunk. Participating in this graphic freak show at the tender age of fifteen, I'm lucky I didn't wind up in a psych ward. (But given some of the online fetishes we see today, had I recorded this I may have made a fortune from it! I can see it now—www.jurkey.com, ha-ha!)

When the disturbing "Summer of Turkey Love" ended, I worked part-time at a car wash, then I became a bus boy at a restaurant. The following summer, my friend John Jakubek helped me get a job in a factory that made parts for U-Haul. The gig was monotonous, hot, and noisy, and featured a thick fog of exhaust fumes created by the many machines. Fortunately, the money was very good.

In my junior year of high school, I got a part-time job at a Rite-Aid Drug Store stocking shelves, unloading trucks, working the cash register, and performing any other chore that might be needed. The manager, Joe, took a liking to me and, gradually, he gave me more and more responsibility. Joe taught me how to order merchandise, schedule cashiers, and do the store deposits. He also stressed how important it was to keep the store looking good by pulling all the stock on the shelves forward. Joe would go home early and leave me in charge. I had keys to the store and felt like the lead character in *Titanic*. I was the "king of the world."

When summer came, Joe gave me full-time hours and had me running the place. Then Joe stopped coming in. He said, "Andy,

I will be off next week, so you're in charge." I was seventeen years old and managing a drug store. Five days later, he came back and said, "You're doing great, Andy." Then I did not see him for another week.

The regional manager, Ed, unexpectedly stopped in a couple of times and always had the same question. "Where is Joe?"

I said, "He is off today."

"Will he be in tomorrow?"

"I think so," I said. Ed seemed very irritated, as this was the second time this had happened. My thoughts were that the summer was just about over, and I'd be starting my senior year in school in a couple weeks, so I was not going to let any of this bother or upset me.

The next day, Ed fired Joe and thanked me for running the store. He asked me how much I was being paid. I said, "Two twenty-five an hour." He gave me a seventy-five-cent raise on the spot and asked if I could train a new manager. The next day, I started training a new manager. I continued as a part-timer there during my senior year in high school. From Joe, I learned the value of delegating authority, and more importantly, if you're going to delegate, make sure you cover your butt (ha-ha!).

After graduation from high school, I was offered a full-time summer job at the U-Haul factory for even more money. I said yes and bye-bye to the drug store because I did not want to work nights and weekends anymore. I decided to attend community college in September. (My intended major? Animal husbandry—what else? *Not*.)

I worked part time at a men's clothing store in my two years at community college. I enjoyed my 2 years there. I was very thankful for the experience, (especially for being on the baseball team), I had majors ranging from business to physical education. I was not sure what path to take. I just knew from experience that I did not want to work at a factory, drugstore, or turkey farm.

After two years of college, I took a year off from school to make a few bucks and decide where to focus my energies.

One of the first jobs I had was toiling on a road crew, and after a month I felt that this type of work was not for me. Next, I got hired as an orderly for the emergency room at St. Mary's Hospital in Langhorne, PA. I was curious about this type of work and thought it would be a good introduction into the medical field. I took patients' vital signs when they arrived in the ER and assisted the staff in various ways. I worked the night shift from 11:00 p.m. to 7:00 a.m. On my very first night, an elderly patient came into the ER and passed away.

The head nurse came up to me and said, "Andy, the orderly's job is to take her body to the morgue. Welcome to the ER."

The morgue! Suddenly, I missed the turkey farm!

After a few months, they offered me the orderly job for the operating room. I accepted and was moved to the day shift, with a raise. It was a great learning experience on so many levels. I have the utmost respect for nurses, doctors, and hospital personnel—they're true heroes. After a few months in my new role at the hospital, I decided to try something else.

I was offered a job as a carpenter's helper building houses, and I enthusiastically said yes. I enjoyed the work and camaraderie with the crew. I was up on roofs, hammering and carrying wood and other materials all day. I liked being paid to work outside and get a nice tan at the same time.

A couple of months later I sustained a wrist injury on the job, which put me in a cast for three weeks. You may think that an injury like that is a bad thing; no, it was a blessing in disguise. While my wrist healed, I was offered a job at a summer camp as a counselor. The cast came off and I took the job. I decided to try it because I love kids and consider myself to be a big kid half of the time anyway. This was my chance to see what it would be like. I oversaw a dozen third-grade boys, and I got to coach the softball team. It proved to be a total and complete joy. At the end of the summer, I said, "OK, I'm going back to college to be an elementary school teacher."

Had I not hurt my wrist, I would not have had the opportunity to work in the summer camp, which opened my eyes to how much I really enjoy working with children. I went on to earn a degree in elementary education, becoming the first person in my family to have a bachelor's degree. I also landed a job as a sixth-grade teacher at a school just twenty minutes from home. The icing on the cake was to see my grandmother's face light up because her dream had been to see her children and grandchildren succeed. These various work experiences taught me how important it is to *like and enjoy* what you focus energy on every day.

LOVE AND LAUGHTER

As you may have guessed, comedy is one of my great loves. Do you love to laugh too? If you like comedy, especially if you like Jay Leno (of *The Tonight Show*) or Kevin James (known for his roles in the TV series *King of Queens* and the movie *Mall Cop*), you'll enjoy what's to follow.

Laughing has been a big part of my life as far back as I can remember. When I was a kid, my sister Nina and I would take turns making each other laugh. We simply called the game "Laughs." In college, my buddies and I played the game. Making friends crack up on command was total craziness that led to explosive laughter. Have you heard the term "laughing like a hyena?" That's what it was—to the absolute *max!*

Here's a **life lesson,** courtesy of scientists: laughter is good for you! The Mayo Clinic's research proves that hearty laughter relieves tension and stress. Laughter also boosts the immune system. Additionally, laughing decreases stress hormones and increases immune cells and infection-fighting antibodies, thus improving your resistance to disease. Every study ever done on this topic produces the same results: laughing is beneficial for you. I think you'll agree that laughing is also cheaper than visits to the doctor and pricey medications. Laughter is the best medicine.

In Norman Cousins's 1979 book *Anatomy of an Illness,* he tells a true story about the healing power of laughter. He was diagnosed with an incurable disease and set out to cure himself using laughter. He showered himself with funny movies, books, and comedians. The "medicine" worked, and he totally recovered. How amazing is that? My advice is to look for ways to laugh every day. Get a daily dose of laughter and you'll be doing yourself a lot of good.

I love to laugh, and I love the feeling and the sound of laughter. I especially enjoy being in a room full of people laughing. I call it "laugh therapy." While I was teaching, my passion for laughing led me to start doing stand-up comedy. Being a teacher and having weekends and summers off was perfect to explore such an endeavor.

In the summer of 1978, I found various open stage nights. Even though I had only been on stage a few dozen times, while visiting my friend Mitch Bigos in California, I went to a comedy club called the Newport Laff-Stop Comedy Club. I walked up the manager and said I was a comic from Philly and asked for an unpaid five-minute guest spot, and he said "no." I stayed for the show and decided to come back the next night. I walked up to the manager again, and said "hi, I how about a five-minute guest spot for a Philly comic tonight?" He said," OK"

I did a five-minute routine and got a couple of laughs. Who followed me on the stage, you may be wondering. None other than David Letterman (his *Late Show* would not premiere on NBC until 1982). David was very funny that night (thanks, no doubt, to my stellar warm-up). The closing act on the show was Jay Leno. At that time, Leno had only appeared as a guest on *The Tonight Show* a couple of times but, as a comedy maven, of course, I caught both of his performances. Jay was *hilarious!*

Letterman seemed very unfriendly. If you and I ever meet (I would place those odds at a thousand to one), ask me to do my David Lettermen impression. Jay Leno, on the other hand, was welcoming, awesome, and supportive, and gave me great feedback on my stand-up. One tip he shared: you can guarantee one laugh if you always make sure your mom is in the audience. The very next night Jay was a guest on *The Tonight Show* (then starring Johnny Carson). I went to the taping and got myself invited backstage to say hi to Jay, even though we had just met the night before. This was so cool.

Again, being a teacher and having nights, weekends, holidays, and summers off allowed me time to pursue stand-up and acting. I made numerous trips to New York City to get on stage and perform with some outstanding comedians: Jerry Seinfeld, Larry Miller, Paul Riser, Bill Maher, Bob Nelson, and Joe Bolster to name a few. If we ever meet—by now I'm sure you know the odds—and you're interested in an amazing Jerry Seinfeld stand-up story, I'd be happy to share it with you. For a small fee, of course.

That summer of 1979, I also had the pleasure of performing at Richie Minervini's Eastside Comedy Club in Huntington, NY, on Long Island. The closing act was Eddie Murphy, one of the best comics ever. When he was onstage, the walls shook from the pounding waves of laughter. Off stage, the contrast was amazing; he seemed like a shy kid. A year later, he would be on *Saturday Night Live*.

In 1980, after three years of teaching, I decided to commit to comedy and acting full-time. I started a comedy production company, Comedy Cabaret, www.ComedyCabaret.com which would partner with area restaurants, nightclubs, and hotels to present the shows. I was told by more than a few people that comedy shows were not going to work in the Philadelphia area. Some even said it was a stupid idea. They said no one would come to see comedians who were unknown. I was told that if by chance it did work, it would only be temporary, and the fad would burn out in less than five years. I still own Comedy Cabaret. So how long have we been in business? You do the math. (I'd do it myself, but I'm not sure in what year you're reading this book.)

Life lesson: when you want to do something, set a goal and do it! Never let people talk you out of it. Unless, of course, you want to do something illegal; then you can listen to the people who will try to talk you out of it. Say "no" to anything illegal.

I hired Jay Leno to perform at my Comedy Cabaret in 1982. After Jay became the host of *The Tonight Show,* in 1992, whenever I was in California, I'd take in one of his shows, and I was given the VIP treatment. In the early nineties, I worked with some great comedians, Kevin James, Joe Rogan, Ray Romano, Bill Maher, and Brian Regan at my Comedy Cabaret venues. These men were not only outstanding comedians but were great guys off stage as well.

I especially love comic/actor Kevin James, whom I mentioned earlier. Besides being known for TV's *King of Queens* and the movie *Mall Cop*, he also starred in *Grown Ups, Hitch, Zookeeper, Here Comes the Boom,* and many others. In 2014, about ten years after he played at my comedy clubs, he made a shout-out video for Comedy Cabaret. Aptly titled "Kevin James Endorses Comedy Cabaret," the twenty-four second YouTube video is Kevin saying hello and recommending our comedy shows. He was making about $20 million per movie then, yet he still took the time to support an old friend. *You have to love that!* If you ever meet Kevin—million-to-one odds—he'll tell you all about the Comedy Cabaret video. Here is the link: https://www.youtube.com/watch?v=G5kOJLdR3GI. It's also available on the *Comedy Cabaret Comedy Club* YouTube channel.

From the mid-'80s to the mid-'90s I also did a lot of acting work. I appeared in more than a dozen local TV commercials and industrial films in the Philly market, and then, in 1993, I landed a part on FOX TV's *America's Most Wanted,* playing a police officer. There was some talk of me winning an Emmy for that performance, but I told my mom to calm down. After this local thespian success, I decided to move to New York City and enroll in acting classes at the Lee Strasberg Method Acting School. It was early 1994. I wanted to see what it was like to study acting in the Big Apple.

By the end of August of 1995, I decided the acting route was not what I wanted, and I was very comfortable with this decision. A couple of weeks before I would be moving back to Philly, I saw a sign for a one-night seminar called "Success with Self-Hypnosis." I registered. Little did I know it was going to be the start of something *big*.

:)

SO HOW DID I BECOME A HYPNOTHERAPIST?

Did you ever have an experience where you step back and ask yourself, "How did I get here?"

***

In 1995 I would *never* go to a hypnotist, *no way*, because I saw the movies about hypnotists and did not want anyone controlling my mind. I was, however, very curious about it. The only reason I attended my first self-hypnosis seminar is because it said *self*. I'm thinking, *Self-hypnosis? OK, I can do that.*

The instructor, a confident man in his early sixties, was Dr. Barry Seedman. The very first lesson in the seminar was *all hypnosis is self-hypnosis*. What? This means it's up to *you* to accept what's being said.

At the end of the self-hypnosis seminar, which I enjoyed very much, Dr. Seedman announced that he would be teaching a basic hypnotist certification course the following weekend and he had a few seats left. He specifically said, "Even if you don't have any desire to be a hypnotist, if you just want to learn more about hypnosis, it would be worth it." As I said earlier, I had *no* interest in being a hypnotherapist. I just wanted to gain knowledge to enhance my own skills at *self*-hypnosis, I had that weekend free, and I had the money, so I signed up.

The seminar room was filled to the brim with people interested in this topic. It was an interesting and eye-opening three-day weekend experience. I quadrupled my knowledge about the hypnosis process. At the end of the weekend, everyone was handed a certificate that said, "You're a Certified Basic Hypnotist."

"Ha!" I laughed to myself, "I'll never use this certificate." Since the certification class gave me a better understanding of what hypnosis was all about, I decided to make an appointment with Dr. Seedman to experience a one-on-one session for myself. It was a very positive experience for me.

Out of the blue, a little over a month after the class, I received a phone call from Dr. Ken Boulden, a practicing hypnotherapist whom I'd known from my comedy business when he was a stand-up comic. Unbeknownst to me, someone in my comedy production office told him that I had completed the basic certification course.

He said, "I heard you received your basic certification."

Then he asked, "How would you like to come to my office and sit in while I see clients?"

My response was immediate: "Why would I want to do that?" He replied, "It's really interesting to work one-on-one with people. You should come see what it's like. I think you'll find it amazing."

I was curious and said, "OK."

A few days later, I found myself sitting next to Dr. Ken, observing as he met with his clients. (You may notice I said *clients*, not patients. My hypnosis instructors taught us that medical doctors see patients, and hypnotherapists work with clients). After the third client, Dr. Ken leaned over and asked me, "Do you want to take the next client?"

I had not anticipated that question. I thought I was just there to observe. I considered it and replied, "Hmm. OK."

The next client was a middle-aged man with a self-esteem issue. I started talking with him about his specific situation and what he wanted to achieve. Words flowed simply and easily from my mouth as we spoke. I guided him into the hypnotic state.

I felt laser-focused, like I was "in the zone." If you've ever played a sport and had one of those games where everything is going perfectly, that's what it felt like. It was almost as if I didn't have to consciously think about what I was saying. The next thing I knew, the session (about an hour) was over, and the client felt great and left the office feeling happy.

Dr. Ken was ecstatic. He shook my hand, looked me in the eye, and said, "You're a natural, Andy. I loved how you slowly guided him into the hypnotic state; your visual reinforcements and the future pacing were very effective. You were fantastic. *Great job!* How would you like to fill in for me one day a week?"

Then I realized why he wanted me to come to his office: he needed help. I enjoyed the session and said, "Sure!"

The next week, I started filling in for him. When I would arrive at his office, a cozy, six-by-eight-foot hypnosis office, which consisted of a recliner, a very small desk, and a chair, there would be a list of names on his desk and what time they were scheduled. It did not say what they wanted to work on. During my second day at his office, a Wednesday afternoon, November 15, 1995, sitting directly across from me was a thirty-five-year-old woman named Shirley.

She was the fourth and last client of the day. We made small talk. Then she looked me in the eye and said, "I have severe lower back pain, and because my orthopedic doctor said the X-rays showed nothing abnormal, he recommended that I see a hypnotherapist."

After only having had a weekend basic course, I didn't know a specific protocol for assisting someone with a pain issue. I did not let her know that. I remained calm, excused myself, and went to call Dr. Ken for some guidance.

Dr. Ken coached me on the phone: "Regress her back to an earlier time when she was pain-free, bring that pain-free feeling to today, and project it into tomorrow." Regression is a hypnotic technique that takes you back in your memory to an earlier time in your life.

I regressed Shirley back to a time when she was pain-free. Then I suggested that this pain-free feeling was with her right now, at this moment, and that she would feel well and pain-free tomorrow as well. I also included suggestions of feeling calm, confident, and strong. We did an hour-long hypnosis session. Afterward she stood up, placed her hands on her lower back, and exclaimed with glee, "Oh my! The pain is gone." She felt *pain-free* and had a big smile on her face. What? She *was?* I felt like one of those faith healers on Sunday morning TV shows, who touch someone and thunderously exclaim, "You're healed!" I was surprised (but did not show that) and amazed and felt very happy that she was better. She was my last client of the day, and as I was walking to my car, I said to myself, "This is positively amazing. I'm going to do this. I'm going to help people."

As I was driving home that day, my car phone rang. It was a good friend. He said, "How are you doing?"

I answered, *"Great*, I'm going to be a hypnotherapist!"

"You're going to be a *what?*"

"I decided to open a hypnosis office; I'm going to do hypnotherapy work."

He said, "Ha-ha, right! And I'm going to be an astronaut."

How did this happen? How did I get here?

***

Just a couple of weeks earlier, if you'd told me I was going to be a successful hypnotherapist, you would have seen me cough up my beer through my nose, and I don't even drink beer. Hypnotist? *No way!* After all, you've probably heard stories about hypnotists making people cluck like chickens, crow like roosters, and walk like ducks. (With those credentials, you would think the job was more suitable to the poultry industry!)

We all know that if there's a hypnotherapist in a movie, it's practically guaranteed that he or she's up to no good. When children are asked, "What do you want to be when you grow up?" No one—*no one*—ever answers, "A hypnotist." Putting that last joke aside, I'm one hundred percent happy with the rewarding work of hypnotherapy and wellness coaching.

Let's get back to Shirley. She was pain-free. How did this happen? At that point I had very limited training in hypnotherapy. Was her subconscious mind so strong that it could erase pain? The answer is "yes," and hypnosis can also assist you in letting go of emotional pain, including fears and phobias. It can also help you erase any unwanted mental habit.

As I said earlier, I had no intention of being involved in this type of work. However, this event profoundly changed my life. I fell head over heels in love with the practice of using hypnotherapy to help people move forward.

I made two decisions that day: I'm going to be a hypnotherapist and, to successfully accomplish that, I need to educate myself to the max and learn everything about hypnosis so I will be able to help whoever is sitting in front of me.

I needed to set up a hypnosis office. Like magic, the universe handed me one. Just one week earlier, the landlord of the building in which my comedy production office was located had offered me the adjacent office space for practically nothing. He could not find a tenant (probably because the thermostat was shared by the spaces). He said, "I will only charge you $100 a month. You could easily charge $200 if I could find someone to sublet it." I knew someone who might be looking for an office, but when that didn't work out, I put an ad in the local paper to rent the space.

The very day after working with Shirley, I arrived back at my comedy office; a man had responded to my ad and left a voicemail saying he wanted that space. I said, "I'm sorry, someone else already took it." That someone was *me*. Had he contacted me just twenty-four hours earlier, I would have sublet the space and would not have had my new hypnosis office. Incredible timing.

With office space obtained, I immediately began learning every- thing possible about hypnosis and mind-changing techniques. I wanted to be able to handle any situation a client might present. I signed up for an advanced hypnosis course in New York City. Dr. Ken gave me complete access to his hypnosis library. I also registered for and attended the largest hypnosis convention in the United States, hosted by the National Guild of Hypnotists. After I earned my advanced degree, in 1996 I enrolled in a doc- toral program through the American Institute of Hypnotherapy in Irvine, California. In 1998, I successfully became a board- certified doctor of clinical hypnotherapy. The American Institute of Hypnotherapy opened in 1988 and was approved to offer a PhD in hypnotherapy. In 2007, the California laws changed, and the school no longer offered the doctorate program. I sure was fortunate to get in when I did!

After transforming my office space into an adequate hypno- therapy office, I started telling everyone I knew that I was open and ready to help, and I did some advertising. Clients started trickling in. A few weeks later, I helped a twenty-five-year-old real-estate agent become a nonsmoker. Several months after that, his dad, a local medical doctor, called and wanted to meet me. Dr. Lawrence Schmitzer began referring clients: a parade of people who needed help with quitting smoking, losing weight, and dealing with stress and anxiety. My practice started getting busy.

Then I received a call from someone wanting to hire a stage hyp- notist for a private party. Since I'd been a stand-up comic, learn- ing to present a stage hypnosis show sounded like it would be easy. I studied stage hypnosis under the legendary Jerry Valley. It turned out to be a lot of fun as well. I began booking shows at private events, comedy clubs, and companies. I performed for Nextel, Johnson & Johnson, Toll Brothers, and Amquip Corporation.

A few years later, Philadelphia's ABC TV news affiliate did a piece about how I was combining my clinical work with my stage show, promoting me as someone who helped people overcome fears, phobias, and stress by day and used the same skill to entertain people by night. The reporter came to my office to experience a professional hypnosis session, during which I suggested that he would not remember his last name when he closed out the segment. It was very entertaining, to say the least (watch on https://www.youtube.com/watch?v=K73k7bEXyQE or see my website). After the segment aired, my practice exploded; I started booking clients a month in advance.

Looking back on how this all unfolded, it's almost as if the universe said, "You should be doing hypnosis work." I was not considering a hypnotherapy profession (I was just curious and wanted to learn self-hypnosis), but then Dr. Boulden invited me to sit in with his clients, and I helped Shirley, which triggered a decision to become a hypnotherapist. The good news continued with the office space being handed to me, then a local medical doctor sending referrals, a request for a private show, and beginning to do stage hypnosis shows, which led to corporate events. I earned a doctorate. The local news did a feature on my work— wow! What a wonderful journey. And now, you are reading my book! (Thank you for that.)

I then had a request for life and wellness coaching and began offering that as well. I had studied nutrition in college and was interested in what supplements might be beneficial. At the time, my hypnosis practice was doing very well.

In 2002, I was crazy busy, with hypnosis clients, and still running my other business (Comedy Cabaret); plus, I was always coaching one of my son's various teams. I was going nonstop seven days a week. I started to feel run down and tired. I said to myself, "I cannot be tired." I thought I was eating healthy; little did I know how bad the standard American diet is for us (SAD).

I was experiencing constant fatigue, brain fog, and gut issues. I just kept pushing and pushing myself until the experience became all encompassing; it was difficult to do anything. I had always been the person who was full of energy. Now it was challenging to just lift my head. Over the next year, I would see seven different doctors in three different states. They had me on four types of medication. None of them worked. My weight went from 165 to 140. One doctor told me I needed to have my gallbladder out. (Fortunately, I did not listen to him, and I still have it.) All the doctors could tell me was, "You have chronic fatigue syndrome." I actually thought to myself, *I'm going to die young.*

Obviously, my life was put on hold. Have you ever heard the expression "like a limp washcloth?" That was me. I was absent from work, family functions, social events, vacations, weddings, and so on. After a year of getting nowhere, I tried alternative medicine. I worked with a marvelous woman; her name was Korine. She had studied Chinese medicine in China. The treatments consisted of acupuncture, Tuina, which is a type of massage along your meridians, and herbal remedies. I was also instructed to make a daily morning smoothie with kale, ginger, parsley, garlic, and lemon; I was told to avoid standard American pasteurized milk and cheese. I was seeing Korine three times a week for the treatments, and after a few months, I started to feel a bit better. Then the treatments were cut down to two times a week and after a few more months, I continued to feel even better. From that point, I worked with Korine once a week for a couple more months and finally, *finally* by the end of the year I was feeling like myself again. (FYI, Korine is now retired. I'm so thankful for her help at that time in my life.)

During this recovery period, I also connected with Dr. Bruce Lewandowski who's a chiropractor and also practices nutritional muscle testing (NRT). This is a really cool technique that uses your body as an energy system to determine what makes your body strong or weak. NRT allows your body to communicate where imbalances are occurring and identify the potential causes. I was using NRT to determine which supplements would be most beneficial and it really helped.

What I'm about to tell you next, even I could not believe! I was finally back to my full schedule, and I was experiencing a toothache. My dentist told me I needed a root canal and to schedule it. Well, on my next visit to Dr. Bruce Lewandowski, I mentioned the toothache and root canal my dentist wanted me to have. He tested the tooth with the NRT and confirmed that the tooth was causing a weak point for my system. Then he put a supplement in my hand that tested strong as a remedy for the toothache.

What? A supplement for a tooth problem? Yes, that is what NRT can do—it can zero in on any issue. Dr. Bruce suggested I take the supplement that I tested positive for. Now wait until you hear this—the supplement was made from the pulp of pigs' teeth. Yum, yum! I know it sounds crazy, but I figured, *what the heck, let me try it*. The NRT test said I needed six of these supplements a day. So, I started taking them. After a couple of weeks, it still hurt, but not quite as much, and Dr. Lewandowski said to just stick with it. A little over a month later, the pain was gone. *Gone!* I never had the root canal. And remember: the dentist said, "You need a root canal!" That was 2004. I became an ardent believer in the NRT process.

What did I learn from all of this? Root canals may not be necessary and may contribute to numerous health issues. Recently, I had an old root canal removed because it became infected. Medical doctors, who have good intentions, aren't necessarily in tune with getting to the origin of your problem. They treat the symptoms. Their answer is usually prescription medication. At this point in my life, I would recommend a functional medicine doctor since they're trained to get to the root cause of the problem and address it.

I have also learned that you must educate yourself on health protocols that truly work.

During COVID, when I had a lot of free time, I began researching ways to maximize my health to increase my longevity. I read over a dozen books. If you would like to feel physically and mentally great, you need to be in control of your mind and keep your overall health as a priority. Here are my health notes for you:

- First and foremost, prioritize your mental and physical health.

- Eat the right foods. Say *no* to the crap foods. Sugar is poison. Ultra-processed foods are poison. The standard American diet is mostly ultra-processed foods that are killing us and making us weak and sick. Starchy carbohydrates are unhealthy for you. One bagel equals nine teaspoons of sugar. One can of soda equals nine and a half teaspoons of sugar. Potato chips, white rice, white bread, refined pasta, sugary breakfast cereals are truly unhealthy, and making us weak and sick. My suggestion is to keep them out of your mouth.

- Eat organic whole foods as much as possible.

- Practice healthy sleep hygiene. All of today's health gurus agree that good sleep is the foundation of good health. For optimum sleep, don't eat for four hours before bed. Also, the blue light emanating from your mobile device and computers are bad news for us close to bedtime. That frequency of blue light tells our brain it needs to be awake. Use blue-light blocking glasses at night. The recommendation is to turn off all screens a couple of hours before bed.

- Get outside and get some sun and fresh air. Get morning light. This helps set your circadian rhythm patterns and helps you sleep better.

- Get your body moving. Exercise is better for us than any supplement we could ever take. Keep your body moving on a regular basis.
- And, of course, look for ways to laugh and love!

My top five health books that I recommend include:

- *Grain Brain* by David Perlmutter
- *Gut Check* by Dr. Steven Gundry
- *The Wahls Protocol* by Dr. Terry Wahls
- *The Glucose Goddess Method* by Jessie Inchauspe
- *Genius Foods* by Max Lugavere

Thank you for sharing my journey. My work has given me the opportunity to assist thousands of people, help them to feel better about themselves, attain their goals, and enjoy their lives to the fullest. I love that! Now, twenty-nine-plus years later, I happily share my insights, knowledge, and life experiences as a hypnotherapist, coach, father, and businessman to help you reach your goals and enjoy your life to the fullest. I hope you gained some insight and knowledge that will have you feeling positive and great about yourself and life!

Life lesson: Be open to change and opportunities, my friend. The times when I said "yes" to new experiences are what led me to a whole new career.

Thank you for reading this book, and always remember you have a powerful mind—keep it on the positive track! God Bless.

ACKNOWLEDGMENTS

Maximum gratitude to my bestie, my soulmate, my number one teammate, my beautiful bride Marilyn, whose love, support, and good humor are fuel to my fire. This book would not have happened without her massive cuteness and editing skills.

Speaking of editing, a big round of applause for my other editors. Thank you, Laura Pasquale and the editing team at American Real Publishing.

Special thanks to my mom: I would not be who I am today without the unconditional love of my mom and my grandmother, two amazing women that I have been blessed with. My mom is still going at ninety-three. Love you, Mom.

Gratitude is one of the best attitudes! I'm so thankful to all of those who came before us. I'm especially grateful to all four of my grandparents, who, in the 1920s, made the voyage from Italy across the Atlantic Ocean through Ellis Island, New York, so that I could be born in the United States. That was about a hundred years ago. Did you ever think about what life was like just one hundred years ago? We now have an unprecedented amount of information at our fingertips. There are more medical advances, more scientific discoveries, and more opportunities now than ever before. This is the greatest time in the world to ever be alive.

And a heartfelt thank you to my three successful children, Laura, Mike and Joe, whom I love and adore. You've brought more joy and happiness into my life and have helped make me a better person in more ways than I can say. Lots of love for my favorite son in-law Matt Dorsey and my two beautiful daughters-in-law Paige and Cara.

I'm also blessed to have two wonderful sisters, Nina and Andi; who also have wonderful husbands, Michael Wommack and Jonathan Mosenson. A big thank you to my uncle Johnny Medaglia, who was very supportive to me as a young boy when I needed it most. And his lovely wife, my aunt Pat, who was always supportive and loving. And thank you to my beautiful niece, Sharon Grosso, and my nephew, Nathan. And thank you to the mother of my two children, Laura and Mike, Dr. Deb Scarpati, who has always been an excellent co-parent. And my brother and sister-in-laws *rock*—Bruce and Joann Peck, Scott and Alice Peck, and Steve and Joann Peck.

For my *hypnosis teachers,* my appreciation is off the charts. First and foremost, thank you, Dr. Ken Boulden. Without his encouragement and advice there would be no Dr. Scarpati. I'm also a big fan of these hypnosis instructors, Barry Seedman, PhD; Gerald Kine; Jerry Valley; Don Mottin; Laura Amoroso; Mike Leggy; Phil Holder, PhD; and Richard Neves, PhD. I'm very grateful to my fellow hypnotherapy practitioners and coaches, who are out there helping others.

I have also been blessed with the guidance of many other teachers and coaches. Thank you to the late Fred Gerst; Ed "Pop" Riley; and James Silver. And a special thank-you to Dr. Lawrence Schmitzer and author Pat Rocchi.

Thank you, thank you, thank you to the authors who have enlightened me in my personal growth and evolution. I applaud, with a standing ovation, the following: Claude M. Bristol, Fran Capo, Deepak Chopra, Joe Dispenza, Wayne Dyer, Victor Frankl, Michael Greger, David R. Hawkins, J. Martin Kohe, Louise Hay, Og Mandino, Norman Vincent Peale, Tony Robbins, Thomas Sugrue, Eckhart Tolle, Doreen Virtue, and Denis Waitley, to name a few.

Tons of gratitude and love to my many friends and mentors with whom I have traveled through life. The following wonderful humans have helped me with my business endeavors or have encouraged me, or, just as important, *have made me laugh!* Thank yuzus go to Rick Hegyi, Evan Dakis, Sally Dakis, Mitch Bigos, Ed Riley, Maureen Riley, Terry Gillespie, Joe Bolster, Pete Lukocheck, Roland Lukocheck, Todd Glass, Carole Connelly, Bob "Oscar" Mayer, Pat O'Donnell, Mary Fan Connelly, Ted Kelly, Fran Capo, Paul Lyons, Taylor Mason, Bob Nelson, Rich Minervini, Grover Silcox, Rich Shidner, Joe Conklin, Bob Alper, Michael Baldwin ("The Wid"), Michael O'Connell, Maria Gannon, Dr. Bruce Lewandowski, Karen Clift, Darin Martinez, Jamie McWilliams, John Jakubek, Pete Styer, Blaine Greenfield, J. J. Ramirez, Wayne Cauble, Doug Esch, Michelle Letvenko, Craig Trostle, Ray Harper, Jeff Sussman, Amir Golan, Tracy Locke, Gabe Abelson, Big Daddy Graham, Tony Conaway, Marlon Martinez, Kevin James, Jay Leno, Steve Young, Mel Kardos, Vinnie Mark, Mike Eagan, John Kensil, Troy Moore, Joey Callahan, Bill Chaing, Coleman Green, Scott Baker, Jennifer Espenshade, Dennis Blaszcyk, Rick Lombardi, Al Isaacs, David Graham, Helene Angley, Missy Hall, Jeremy Hall, Gene Norris, Debbie Kasper, Sheila Kay, Chris Coccia, Dena Blizzard, Belynda Clarie, Brad Lowery, Chris Monty, Jay Black, Donna Ottena, Romont Harris, Dan Palucis, Bob Marsdale, Simplee D, Bill Boronkay, Anita Wise, Steve Shaffer, Glenn Freezman, Wayne Cotter, Kevin Tiers, and Tim Conniff.

And some extra gratitude for the good work of MAGIC Charities foundation and OWE Charity, which will receive a percentage of the proceeds from sales of this book.

Last but not least, thank you, Shirley, for having a little back issue in Nov. of 1995 that brought us face to face.

And thank YOU for reading this book!

RECOMMENDED READING LIST

I'll begin this list with my top three books for you, listed in the order I suggest reading them. I discovered the first book, *The Power Is Within You*, when I really, *really* needed it in 1991 while going through a divorce. It felt like a lifesaver.

1. *The Power Is Within You* by Louise Hay
2. *Man's Search for Meaning* by Victor Frankl
3. *Power vs. Force* by David R. Hawkins

A Course in Miracles by Helen Schucman

A Garden of Thoughts by Louise Hay

A Heartfelt Journey by Michael Peck

Anatomy of an Illness by Norman Cousins

Awaken the Giant Within by Tony Robbins

Breaking the Habit of Being Yourself by Joe Dispenza

Breath by James Nestor

Get the Results You Want by Kim Kostere

Great Failures of the Extremely Successful by Steve Young

Gut Check by Steven Gundry

Healing and Recovery by David R. Hawkins

Hopeville by Fran Capo

How Not to Die by Michael Greger

Irreversible by Taylor Mason

Letting Go by David R. Hawkins

Many Lives, Many Masters by Brian Weiss

Metabolical by Robert H. Lustig

Morning Manna: Carpe Diem by Paul Lyons

Self-Hypnosis by Henry Leo Bolduc

Self-Hypnosis Manual by Alman & Lambrou

Thanks, I Needed That by Robert Alper

The Biology Belief by Bruce Lipton

The Eye of the I by David R. Hawkins

The Energy Paradox by Steven Gundry

The Five People You Meet in Heaven by Mitch Albom

The Greatest Miracle in the World by Og Mandino

The Lightworker's Way by Doreen Virtue

The Longevity Paradox by Steven Grundy

The Magic of Believing by Claude M. Bristol

The Power of Positive Thinking by Norman Vincent Peale

The Psychology of Winning by Denis Waitley

The Purpose Driven Life by Rick Warren

The Relaxation Response by Herbert Benson

The Six P's of Change by Pat Rocchi

Truth vs. Falsehood by David R. Hawkins

Unlocking the Keto Code by Steven Gundry

Wisdom of the Ages by Wayne Dyer

You're Not That Pretty by Debbie Kasper

Your Greatest Power by Martin Kohe

www.ingramcontent.com/pod-product-compliance
Lightning Source LLC
Chambersburg PA
CBHW030251130626
46549CB00002B/481